FOURTH EDITION

COLLEGE
TO THE
CAREER
YOU LOVE

KENNETH BUCKLEY
JEFFREY STUBBS
MICHAEL ESTEPP

Kendall Hunt
publishing company

Cover image © Shutterstock, Inc.

Kendall Hunt
publishing company

www.kendallhunt.com
Send all inquiries to:
4050 Westmark Drive
Dubuque, IA 52004-1840

Copyright (c) 2018 by Kenneth Buckley, Jeffrey Stubbs, and Michael Estepp
Copyright © 2014, 2015, 2017 by Kenneth Buckley

ISBN 978-1-5249-7185-4

Published in the United States of America

CONTENTS

ACKNOWLEDGMENTS

This book is dedicated to college students who are trying to make sense of the incredibly challenging and ever changing job market.

The book would have not been possible without the assistance of our career management staff. They always put students first and get up each day with a mission first mentality of helping students realize their career dreams. Amy, Kristy and Tisha thanks for always giving your best. To our wives and kids, thanks for always being our inspiration and encouragement.

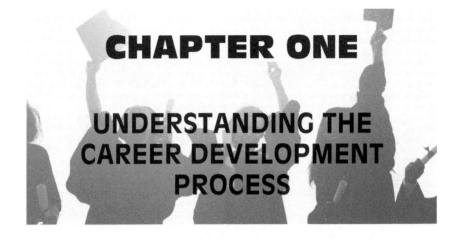

CHAPTER ONE

UNDERSTANDING THE CAREER DEVELOPMENT PROCESS

A s a student, you have many demands on your time and although your career is clearly an important part of your future, most students procrastinate and postpone putting time into their career development. Your career success is an incredibly daunting and challenging issue and it is normal that you would want to postpone something like this until the last moment, where you either have much more information or someone miraculously provides you with the opportunity of your dreams.

I was working with a student about his career direction and trying to help him identify the career role that would be a great fit for him. We spoke at length and I could tell he was struggling to find that perfect role. He was clearly feeling the pressure of this basic career question.

He spoke to me about several things he absolutely did not want to do in his job when he graduated with his undergrad business degree. These items were:

> Did not want to work in a large company environment
>
> Did not want to work in a heavily financial-based industry
>
> Did not want to work exclusively indoors
>
> Did not want to be sitting in front of a computer screen or on the phone all day
>
> Did not want to work 65 hours a week

He also said there were things he wanted to do:

> He did want to help others and make a difference
>
> He did want to earn a decent salary, however money was not the most important thing
>
> He did want to know that his work was appreciated and others sought him for support
>
> He did want to work outdoors at least a portion of time
>
> He did want to have beneficial training and development and be a recognized subject matter expert within his area of responsibility.

I had the benefit of knowing this student personally. If I had not known this student and had only taken his input at face value in order to solve the career role challenge question, I might have suggested the perfect role for him would be a forest ranger in a national forest/park, a store manager in a sporting goods or outdoors-based retail environment or some type of career in a nonprofit or government role. However, buried deeply within this student was his *core interest*, which was to make a difference in others as well as to be recognized as the go-to person for help and support.

The irony of this story is this student accepted a job with a firm that IS a large company and IS in the financial industry. His job IS in a corporate role and he IS in a cubicle and in front of a computer on the phone the majority of his day. His job is Client Relations Coordinator and he loves it. The company he works for has strong faith values and cares deeply about their clients. He is well trained and is the first point of contact to people who have a problem. He is the subject matter expert and he is completely energized by making a difference to the people he interacts with.

Let's look back at what he wanted originally. If I would have asked him to focus on the Client Relations Coordinator job type and to actively apply for it and others like it, he would have fought mightily against it. The reason he would have fought against it is because it was all the things he thought he didn't want in a job. Yet, after learning more about it and accepting the job, it was truly the right fit.

Does this mean that you should just forget any career direction and jump at the first opportunity that comes your way? Absolutely not. But you should have an attitude of flexibility and curiosity. Do not become so wrapped up on what is your perfect career role that you miss opportunities that you will enjoy. After all, we learn far more from having taken the journey than just being at the destination.

The more you understand about your core interest, the better you can position yourself for opportunities. Seek ways to stretch yourself and to push yourself to learn more about what you like and what you do not like. Have an attitude of adventure and curiosity. Students who have this attitude have a much better chance of career satisfaction and enjoyment.

Take heart if you are nervous, anxious, and prone to procrastination due to your fears of potential failure or making a bad career decision. Understanding what really drives you and being open to challenges will help you position yourself for success. Going through this college career survival guide will help you with the fundamentals to discover those core interests and to turn them into a bridge to your career success.

There are simply not many items more important to your professional development than clarity on your career dreams and a game plan to make those dreams a reality. With that said, let's look at the practical aspect of your college career.

For the most part you, or your parents, are paying a large sum of money and you are dedicating years of your life to a process that, on one hand can create incredible fulfillment of your life dreams or on the other hand, can create a huge amount of stress and frustration as you worry about what you are going to do when you graduate. Many college graduates fall into the stressed, frustrated, underemployed, seriously unprepared, or unemployed category. It's a sad statistic considering how much time you will spend in your career over your lifetime. What is sadder is when you realize the potential impact and difference it can make if you are prepared, informed, and accountable. Spending just a few hours a week can be a game changer with respect to realizing your career dreams. Unfortunately, students don't make their career management a priority nor do they take advantage of all the career resources that they have available to them at their colleges/universities. Why is that?

Possible answers:

(A) The career resources seem outdated and ineffective.
(B) Students think they do not have the time to utilize the resources because of other commitments or demands.
(C) The student has a multimillion dollar trust fund, so why worry?
(D) The student is planning to make their career a priority as they get closer to graduation.

The answer most selected is B, followed by D.

Let's dive deeper into your career and college. What is your purpose of going to college? You know you need a college degree to have an improved chance of financial security, but have you honestly researched the career or industry projections in your major field of study? Why are you taking that core class or that elective and why are you enrolled in that major? What is holding you back from having more career awareness and personal accountability? You are ultimately going to be the one that enjoys or that is frustrated by the opportunities that present themselves for an internship or a full-time position once you graduate. You should know or at least have an interest in the industry trends or career projections in your degree field.

My hope is that when you finish this book you will have a much better perspective on your overall career management. You will also better understand the following "questions" and "answers."

Q: "When I get my degree, what do I want to do for the rest of my life?"

A: The answer to this is incredibly hard and isn't specific to job role, company of interest or industry field. It is an answer of attitude.

Q: "Am I preparing myself for success and self-reliance or am I assuming that my career is just going to work out?"

A: While the opportunities for college graduates are increasing in most areas and the potential for professional success is as strong as it has ever been, the majority of students do not take their career interests or career preparation seriously. Nor do they take advantage of the career potential in the improving professional job market.

To be clear, this book will do you no good sitting on your shelf or sitting in your computer's hard drive if you don't honestly make an effort to become more informed about your career and the challenges you will likely face. We want you to understand your potential as well as your need to be personally accountable. To realize your potential you need an honest, straightforward understanding of the career process. This book is your career survival guide and it will help you navigate through the confusion, chaos, and uncertainty of your academic and early professional development.

In order to give you a road map of what to expect with this book and to prepare you accordingly for career success, we segmented the career management process to seven (7) basic career processes.

1) *Understand your interests, your motivation, what drives you and what interests you.*

This discovery process can be assisted by many of the self-assessment tests that are available today. Fortunately, there are numerous Web-based, free or low-cost self-assessments which we would encourage you to utilize. We use a specific career assessment tool for our college students, called CareerLeader. It is not free, but it is reasonable and it is comprehensive. The CareerLeader orientation presentation would tell you that the self-assessment tool is recognized by its ability to identify your core interests, abilities, skills, and motivations as well as identify career paths you will likely enjoy and find success. In addition, the assessment identifies the company organizational culture or environment that you will likely enjoy. It also alerts you to potential career issues where you may have shortcomings. CareerLeader is a great tool and if your university does not provide access to you, it would be worthwhile for you to engage it on your own.

With many of the students we work with, the CareerLeader assessment highlights areas they thought they might be strong in and gives them additional confidence to pursue these areas. It also refines their understanding of the major drivers in their career satisfaction. Think of this stage as a gap analysis. You gain an understanding of where you are and you gain clarity on where you want to be. You also understand the gap between where you are and where you want to be and what is required to turn that gap into a bridge. We consider this step one of the most critical parts of your career development. We know for sure it is probably what many of you struggle with the most. Do not panic, we will go deeper into this section in later chapters.

It is our hope that you come away from these career tools with a much greater sense of clarity and understanding about yourself and how to target careers that will energize you and give you a renewed purpose for making that potential commute to work and back each day.

2) *Target career areas of interest through research.*

This becomes especially challenging when you consider (for the most part) that you have no professional experience in the areas you "think" you are interested in. This would be similar to ordering food from a menu that is written in a foreign language you do not understand. You honestly have no idea what you are ordering until it arrives at your table. You truly do not know if you ordered the house special or something better served on a reality TV show.

Consider your background and work history as again, you most likely have little or no professional experience in the specific career area in which you think you are interested. You want to be a teacher, accountant, coach, CEO, physician, marketing manager, project leader, scientist, biologist, politician, salesman, preacher, entrepreneur, and so on yet, honestly, you really do not know a thing about these roles. How are you going to select something to spend the rest of your life doing when you have actually never done it before? Align yourself to your interests and start there.

In addition to the uncertainty of your career direction, what about the constantly changing job market, highly volatile economy, and the fact that much of your potential job satisfaction could be lost when either the boss you really enjoy working for goes to another company or the group you love to work with is reorganized due to the latest corporate merger and acquisition (M&A). There was even a time where individuals went to work for the government or in education because they felt that was a very steady and stable environment. We know now that the government can actually be downsized and school systems can have their budgets slashed. The only thing that we can depend on in the future is change. We know this does not give you a sense of comfort, but hang in there it will get better. We believe you are far better knowing what to expect when you graduate because you can prepare for it.

So how do you select a career with so many unknowns? You more than likely do not know what you want to do and you, for sure, cannot predict the future; so how do you select your career area of interest? The answer to that is to research career areas and become much more informed on the future development in the fields of interest that you have. In addition, be willing and committed to work a little each day to broaden your employable skills. Continue to develop, evolve, and adapt. We could give you several career fields that are in high demand today such as cyber-security, healthcare medical professionals, data analytics information systems, or consulting, but there are no guarantees these will be booming when you graduate. Also, what might be booming in one region might be declining in the region in which you want to live. So, know going into your career decision that there are no guarantees and many unknowns.

When talking with students, alums, and executives, they often share similar stories about why they selected a particular career or selected an area of personal interest. Think about where you are today with your specific interests. Most individuals play a specific sport, enjoy a specific extracurricular activity, or have an interest in a specific class or major because someone noticed them and encouraged them. The majority of people we have spoken with and talked to do not continue in areas that are especially challenging when they do not experience at least moderate success. True, there are some incredibly determined individuals who keep pushing forward no matter what they face, but the majority will stop soon after they experience struggles. This is important to know and understand, because it helps you select your career interests. It may also help you understand that maybe what you are doing is not what you really want to do, but in fact it is something others want you to do. Please do not misunderstand what we are saying. We are not saying do not listen to those more experienced then you with respect to your career interests (parents, older friends, professors, etc.). What I am saying is, just be clear why you are choosing a particular area. If you are choosing this field for others or at the direction of others, make sure you have at least an interest in it as well as a willingness to give it your best.

When you were in high school, for example, after you selected an interest area in sports, music, school, and so on, you most likely saw progress in that area. It also shows within your respective interest area your ability to adapt, develop, and succeed within that specific area or areas. When you pick the sport, musical instrument, class, hobby, or activity, it is very similar to selecting a career field. You select it, then work at it, get better through work and dedication and become more proficient, and if you are willing to work hard enough you may rise to the top of your field. As with most things, the better you become the more satisfied you are. It is important that you are able to look at yourself in the mirror and be excited you selected your career field. Just know that a good decision comes after preparation and do not expect something to miraculously work out for you. You need to dig deep and thoroughly review what you know about yourself and your interests. What we see most often when students struggle in this second process comes from a hesitancy to explore career areas and an even greater hesitancy to make the commitment to give their best and attempt to excel.

One question I ask my students is what would you do if you won the lottery? You win $50 million and you travel, buy some great things, and enjoy yourself. At some point you decide to do something that is meaningful to you. The reason is you no longer have to do something for money. Money is very important to be sure. It is just that if all you want is money, there will never be enough. After you win the lottery and have some fun, you would eventually end up wanting to do "something." You might build something or work with others less fortunate than you, start a business, write, become a musician, or work to create a cure for a disease.

Thinking about these things allows you to dive deep into areas that are truly an interest for you. If we break that down to your career; while you may not be a professional athlete (no matter how much you love it), how exciting would it be to work in the sports industry in some professional capacity? If you want to start a business then working in a start-up to gain experience and a deeper understanding, as well as credibility, would be a perfect scenario for you. Hopefully, you see the point; you can align yourself to your interests. Do not be fooled to think there is only one place for you to work and only one specific role or else you will not be happy or fulfilled. That is just not the case. Always seek career areas that interest you. Research them to be as informed as you possibly can be about the career roles, hiring trends, market influences, and growth projections. Understand what it takes to be successful in these areas and work as hard as you can to be the best in your field of interest. In addition, speak to people who are in this career field and gain a deeper understanding into their roles. Target not only individuals who are doing the job that you hope to do upon graduation but also talk to those that are several levels above. We will talk about how to perform this "contact connection and analysis" later.

3) *Prepare an effective resume and establish your professional brand.*

Many students look at a resume as a chronological, biographical picture of themselves which is fact-based and that is great, but they fail to realize that a resume has but one objective. That objective is to secure an interview. Your resume could tell a wonderful story about you, but if it does not show a strong fit for the opportunity (internship or full-time job) you are seeking you will most likely not be successful securing an interview. A simple way to verify that your resume shows a strong fit is to identify and select keywords within the opportunity you are seeking under qualification or requirements. Once you identify the keywords then hit Ctrl + "F" with your resume open on your computer screen and see if you have any matches. Sophisticated companies establish formulas or key word searches and scan your resume when you apply. You could be the greatest fit in the world, but if your resume does not show a fit, your resume could go into the "we received your resume and thank you for your application, but at this time we have selected more qualified candidates" trash can. We will spend time on your resume and other tactical career skills later in the book.

Many students ask if they can use the same resume when applying for different jobs. If the jobs are the same, then the answer is yes. However, since that is highly unlikely, you need to modify, reframe, adjust and refocus your resume to each opportunity. Also be sure to use your name in the file name, otherwise the recruiter or hiring manager may have difficulty finding you. Do not title your resume file "Resume," but instead title it with your name, the company name, the date you applied and possibly the job I.D. Remember that it must show a strong fit or your chances of being selected for an interview are slim.

Your professional brand is vital. Today, you may have a strong social media presence but to be taken seriously as someone who is looking for gainful, professional employment you need a LinkedIn page/profile. I spend most of my time with college students and many of them have well-established social presences via Facebook, Instagram, Snapchat and other social media forums. That image may be who you are or who you think you are or who you want to be, but it likely does not represent and articulate why someone would compensate you for working for their company. LinkedIn is actively used by recruiters and hiring managers and this percentage is growing. There will come a time in the near future that a LinkedIn profile may suffice for a resume. There may be new professional social platforms that are even more beneficial than LinkedIn, but at this time, as an entry level candidate into the job market, you must have a LinkedIn profile to be taken seriously. LinkedIn has an excellent Web site for assisting students (Undergrad and Grads) with the development of their LinkedIn profiles as well as how to use all of the LinkedIn resources to maximize their career success.

When you review the LinkedIn profile checklist from the LinkedIn college student development web site, you will see many sections that may seem strange to you. Those sections show a connection to the career area you are interested in. Establishing your profile is only half of the process. The other half is connecting with "influencers." You want to connect with individuals with whom you share a common interest. This could be an alumnus, an individual who is in a specific career or industry area or job function, a person that shares a common experience or connection like working for the same company you worked part-time, co-op or interned with you or your professor, teacher, friend, family, church member, coach, and so on. We will spend additional time on this later in the book.

© Sergey Nivens/Shutterstock.com

4) *You need a strategy for your job or internship search.*

It is easy to apply to jobs and internships on the internet and it is quite ineffective unless you approach it strategically. There are literally thousands of job postings and you can spend a significant amount of time and effort searching for opportunities with little success. Part of your search strategy is breaking down your interest to searchable and distinguishing key words. Search on employer web sites instead of generic catch-all web sites if possible. Specify by location as well to further focus your efforts. If your key word and focus efforts produce the desired results then move forward. If you are not seeing enough opportunities, widen the search. There is a "give and take" with this search strategy as you may have to modify your interests in order to position yourself for success.

If you are interested in working for a small firm, and can't find an open position with a specific employer you will need to modify your search. I would recommend all things being equal that you target a larger more established employer instead of a smaller one. Some might say you should target the smaller firms because you will get a chance to "wear more hats," but while that may be true it is also very likely the employer will have a less sophisticated training and development program, less prestige in the industry, and less interest to a potential employer should you decide to move on to another opportunity. More importantly, securing a position with a large, recognized employer will give you and your resume a "stamp of approval" in the eyes of future employers. If you were looking for new talent to add to your company and all other skills being equal, would you select the person who had 5 years with IBM or 5 years with Bob and Jane's Tech Services? Names, industry reputations, product brands, professional images, performance, and personal experience are all analyzed when you are being evaluated for promotion or hiring.

Your search strategy should take into account positions posted on your university's career web site or career database as well as positions with employers that frequent campus as they often have a vested interest in seeking talent on your campus. Target not only positions that are a strong fit but also companies that employ friends and family members. Keep a spreadsheet of your applications by company, job, or internship title. Include the contact you sent your information to, date of activity, response from the company, required follow-up, interview status, and general comments so you can keep track of and manage your career development actions.

5) *Preparation.*

Let's assume you have made excellent progress in your career development. You now understand your career interests. You know in general terms what you want to do or the functional role you want to play and that you are qualified for (do not forget this very important requirement) in your career and the location or locations that appeal to you. You have an impressive resume that shows a solid fit to the role you desire and you targeted your search so that you represent yourself as clearly a qualified candidate. You also reached out to individuals who know you, or know of you, and can help connect you to the employer you targeted. You did this so that your resume has the greatest chance of being reviewed by a human with decision-making capability. Congratulations. You just received a call from the employer and they want to schedule you for an interview. Preparation becomes critical. Hopefully you have done some research on the company in order to know that this opportunity is a fit for you so that when you begin the interview preparation you are not starting from the beginning.

As a minimum, you need to know the answers to the following critical questions:

- Why do you think this job is a great fit for you?
- Can you articulate why you are the best candidate for the role?

- Why are you attracted to work for this company?
- What is it about this industry that interests you?

There are many other questions you should prepare for, but your mission during the interview is to show that you are energetically interested in and qualified for the position. Another segment of the interview preparation is how you conduct yourself during the interview and how you follow-up after the interview. We will go into greater detail on this later in the book.

6) *Negotiating and conduct during the offer.*

You should be aware of the market value of your degree. We hope before you select your major and establish your degree plan that you research this. Once again, not that money is everything, but understanding this component of your career development is critical to your career satisfaction and your financial budget. You should also be aware of the basic salary and compensation levels for the role you are applying for. You will probably not find the exact amount, but you will gain a good understanding in the salary range by researching salary Web sites like www.glassdoor.com.

You can search salaries by company, location, and by position. There are other salary sites, but this has been a good resource for the students we work with. Another bonus feature of this Web site is that you can also research the company and even the interview process. This is covered in more detail with respect to doing your preparation as discussed in segment five.

7) *What happens after you have accepted the great offer the company makes?*

You have accepted and have an official start date. Chapter seven addresses what you need to do to separate yourself as a performer in the first six months of your job or the first 30 days of your internship. You worked so hard to get to this position; you want to make the best of it, correct? Well, you would be surprised how many recent graduates get the opportunity of their dreams, but within six months to a year they are frustrated and disillusioned with their situation and their new employer is feeling the same way. We will cover these points later.

These seven points are major items in your career development and while we cannot guarantee you a job or internship when you understand and implement them, we can tell you that you are positioning yourself for success to accomplish your career dreams.

© Stephen Coburn/Shutterstock.com

Chapter 1 Review Questions

1. What choice below best describes where you are with respect to your career development?

   a) I don't know what I want to do when I graduate.

   b) I don't know what my options are.

   c) I don't know what career field I would have the most success with.

   d) No need to worry, I still have 4 years to figure it out.

   e) I know what I want to do and I understand what it takes to succeed in that career field.

   f) Other (fill in the blank) _____

   _____

2. The book describes seven major areas in your career management process and progress. List them and then circle the one that you are currently struggling with.

   1.

   2.

   3.

   4.

   5.

   6.

   7.

3. If you won the lottery and suddenly had $50 million to use as you wish, what would you do?

   _____

   _____

   _____

   _____

   _____

   _____

4. Why did you make that choice?

_____

_____

_____

_____

_____

_____

5. When people describe you, which characteristics do they talk about the most?

a)

b)

c)

6. Research career fields that might lead to at least, an entry level role for a college graduate. List three job titles in this career field. These would be for entry level roles for college students.

a)

b)

c)

7. Describe **YOUR** personal "Brand" as if you were talking to a recruiter? _____

_____

_____

_____

_____

_____

_____

_____

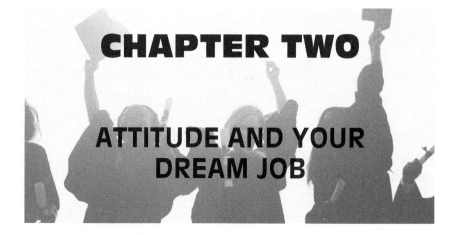

CHAPTER TWO

ATTITUDE AND YOUR DREAM JOB

© ne photo/Shutterstock.com

This may seem like a strange chapter for a career management book, but let us assure you it is at the very core of your career management and, potentially, will contribute more to your success or failure than any other topic we cover in this book. We all love to be in control and we worry and stress about so many things, when actually there are not many things we can control. However, one thing you can definitely control is your attitude. Do not take the previous sentence lightly, it is a powerful thing.

We think everyone has a personal brand (also considered your "reputation") and mission statement. It may not be plastic coated/framed and carried in your purse or billfold or hanging on your wall, but you have it. It is important that you understand your personal brand and mission statement as well as how these things impact your overall attitude. If you only accomplish one thing (we hope you accomplish more) in this book, it will be that you evaluate and then put in writing your personal brand and mission statement. If you are really daring, you will even communicate your personal brand and mission statement to your close friends.

We want you to build your own personal brand. Mine is:

"To every day give my best effort, to be willing to stand up for what is right, and to care about others."

We also want you to have a personal mission statement. Mine is:

"As long as I draw breath, I will give my best, never quit and rejoice in my circumstances."

I believe if you ask people who know me and work with me, they would not be surprised by either statement. I am probably one of the most determined individuals you will ever meet and hence . . . I never quit, and I also rejoice in my circumstances. Rejoicing in your circumstances is probably the greatest challenge of the three items. I trust in a plan and purpose in my life, and I am confident when faced with challenges, adversity, and stress that the greatest thing I can do is push forward and know that no matter what the outcome, I will learn from the experience. I think being able to rejoice in your circumstances also means that you can overcome the fear of failure. This is a critical issue because most of us will not attempt things or even explore things if we are not . . . at least "good" at them. That is why you see so much specialization, including focus as a young person on a single sport or single musical instrument or extracurricular activity. I know if I give my best (even if my best is awful), that is the very best I can do, and we all should be comfortable with that. It sounds simple enough, but if you have done your best, accept your performance and the outcome, and do not be ashamed or embarrassed by it. If you want to improve and become more proficient and accomplished, or you recognize that you need to be better to compete and excel at a higher level, then work at it, practice and push yourself, so that when you give your best again, you will be better. This sounds like it is about your ability, but actually it is all about your attitude.

I do not know if you are a golfer, but this analogy may shed some light on this section. Quite a few golfers are incredibly frustrated (throw their clubs, curse, kick things, scream and shout, and make general fools of themselves) when they do not hit a perfect or even a "solid" shot. I am sure you are familiar with these individuals, and there may be a small chance I just described you. These people expect to play like pros even though they have never spent a reasonable amount of time putting, chipping or working on their drives at a driving range. They only put in a few hours and either end up frustrated that they aren't as good as they expect to be or they give it up altogether because we aren't willing to spend the time to be as good as we want to be.

The attitude I am talking about is one where you clearly recognize that you can only do your best, and if you have not put in any time to practice, your best might be awful. *But . . .* your best is all you can do, and either you decide to practice so that your best becomes better or you enjoy yourself based upon where you are with your skills.

Here is another analogy about the attitude we hope you come to embrace. I am a horrible ice-skater, but when I lived in Massachusetts, I took a church youth group ice-skating, even though I had never ice skated in my life. I fell every time I went around the rink. I mean, You-tube video-type wipeout. Now, I am a decent athlete, and for most of my life, I have had excellent balance, but I was clearly struggling on the ice. It was not pretty, but I knew I was doing my very best each time

I went around the rink. Most of the humans in Massachusetts are well practiced and can skate about the same time they start walking and as such, they found this Texan who wiped out each pass around the ice to be especially entertaining.

I do not know if they were entertained by the impact I placed on my body or the fact that I kept getting up each time and going around again. Their entertainment went from chuckles to laughter, and my very young daughter (who can skate) was so mad at everyone for laughing at her dad she was in tears. She was ready to take the whole house on and could not understand why her dad would subject himself to so much embarrassment and be fine as the center of everyone else's humor.

The answer I told her was that I know that nobody on that rink was working as hard as I was to get better and that I was 100 percent confident I was doing my best. True it was awful, but it would clearly not get any better unless I worked at it. I think most individuals would have retired from ice-skating after the first or second wipeout, but that is just not me. Like I said earlier, I am a determined guy, and in my mind I know everyone else who started skating also struggled. Maybe they spaced out their learning (and impact with the ice) over a few weeks or months, but for me I was trying to learn in one afternoon.

I had to accept the possibilities of failure until I succeeded. I was fine with this and accepted the possibility. In fact, embrace failure if possible, and use it as fuel to keep your motor running and help drive you to levels beyond your expectations. I could have complained, quit, or blamed my lack of success on others or I could "rejoice in my circumstances" and just give it my very best. If you do that, you have to be OK with the outcome. You always want to be the best, but there is quite a difference from wanting to be the best and being the best. Malcolm Gladwell in his awesome book *Outliers* would tell you it takes 10,000 hours of dedicated and focused practice to be truly exceptional at something.

I want to challenge you a little bit. In talking to students, one of the frequent comments I get when I ask them about their background is why they stopped doing something they initially enjoyed or participated in. The common reasons: too small, too slow, no time, no money, not talented enough, and so forth. All of these answers/reasons are valid, but I want to encourage you to take a deeper look at your commitment to enjoy life and participate full out in the adventure that stands before you each day.

Do not ever sell yourself short! The greatest force holding you back from success just happens to be the person staring back at you from the mirror in the morning. Our definition of success is reaching your full potential. We want you to have an attitude that allows you not only to dream of your potential and future, but to believe in your ability to make that dream a reality. If you truly put your heart and effort into the development of that potential, it can be a reality.

We know if you work hard and are not afraid of failure or afraid of engaging in challenging learning situations, you will get better improve and gain confidence. Employers are seeking students with a positive attitude and willingness to help others, be accountable as well as honor their commitments. Employers see these attributes as highly desirable characteristics. Many people were looking to find a way to make their professional careers easier, we recommend that you look for challenges, stretch assignments and ways to improve. We want you to believe that if you set your mind on something and that you are truly willing to work at it, you can and will be successful.

© 4Max/Shutterstock.com

Do not be afraid to dream and then . . . do not be afraid of the work required to make that dream a reality. Attitude is critically important, and I can tell you that trying your best, truly giving your best, and being committed to the point of pushing yourself to improve each day will separate you from your peers.

Attitude. How can you get the right one? Here is a brief story on how I learned to have an attitude of optimism and willingness to face fear and failure. One of the things that had a big impact on me was my family upbringing and background. In my family, I was the oldest, and my father had contracted polio at the age of ten. He had a very, very tough life physically. My mom was a loving, and sensitive woman who always encouraged us. I was also blessed with an amazing brother and sister that were always a source of encouragement and support. As I said, my dad had many problems physically such as one foot being a size 7 and the other being a size 9½. He also dealt with the constant pain from the polio that almost took his life at a very young age. These physical and emotional challenges made him one very tough individual.

I would say he fell down often as an adult, probably once or twice a month just walking or stepping off a curb. Each time he fell, he would bounce up and be fine no matter how much blood and skin he left on the concrete. I can remember seeing him fall from my early childhood, and it terrified me. I was so concerned my tough dad would fall and not get up. As I got older, I asked him one day what made him so tough and he said "getting up" no matter how hard you fall. I also asked if he was mad at "life" or God for the physical pain he experienced or the limits his situation had placed on him. He looked at me and said "**in life everyone faces circumstances, challenges, and opportunities, some greater or more challenging than others, and we can rise to our potential or we can fall to our excuses**." I think of those words often and it helps push me forward.

I knew from an early age that I should always give my best, and even when it seemed like my best was not good enough to accomplish the task at hand; I never gave up. It was far better to live life with that sense of adventure and the satisfaction from always giving your best than to think somehow you had saved something for another day . . . especially when in life there are no guarantees of another day. My dad willed himself to excel under the most challenging circumstances and was an accomplished golfer and competitive athlete as a swimmer and boxer. His lower body was tiny and he always had to buy two different sizes of shoes, but his upper body was as strong as a gorilla. He made no excuses and never accepted them, and for him it was all about being "all-in" each and every day. He was a successful businessman, leader in the community, and mayor of our town. He pushed himself daily, and we (as kids) could not very well say we were sick, did not feel good, or some similar excuse when we could clearly see him dealing so courageously with his physical issues.

I had a loving mother who provided the right amount of nurturing along with my dad's tough love, and it was a great upbringing. I do not know what your personal background is. I do know you are shaped by it, whatever it is. I hope it was something that will push you forward in life and give you courage and determination to make the best of your life in this ever-changing and competitive world. If it was not that type of environment, do not despair; you have everything you need within yourself, you just have to have courage to push yourself and realize life is not about shortcuts.

Attitude is great, but how does that help you identify your dream job? We would say this is one of the biggest questions most students have, and often, it is because they are so uninformed on the opportunities that exist. They may have never truly thought of themselves in a particular career. They may have seen parents or relatives or friends doing jobs, but they have for the most part never stopped and done research on what they would like to do and why. We started this chapter talking about attitude. The reason for this is quite simple. If you have an attitude where you see your career as a series of progressive adventures leading towards increased skills and leadership, you will have more career satisfaction than if you are often frustrated because you are not selected as the best among your peers.

Well, a slight exaggeration maybe, but from a generation's perspective, we want everything and we want it now. That type of attitude will really annoy potential employers. They like someone who is action oriented, but they are not enamored with someone who wants what they have not earned. Attitude and your dream job come together as you develop as an employee and as a professional. As discussed in chapter one, it is very hard to know what you want to do when you have most likely not done a professional job that will replicate or be similar to what you will do when you graduate from college.

So how do you identify your dream job? You start identifying your dream job by researching the job market as best as you can by looking at hiring trends, forecasted job growth, long-term viability of the functional role you will be applying to, and then look at the companies you are interested in. With respect to companies, evaluate their competitive strengths and historical ability to grow during challenging times. Talk to friends, family members, alumni and networking contacts who have or had experience in the industries, companies or roles that you seek. Once you have done the research, review job openings with those companies for which you are qualified for based on your degree plan, major, and background. These openings are your dream job! As you apply to the positions and gain interest from recruiters (because you have shown a strong fit with your resume and you have done your homework to discover why this job is right for you, why the company is perfect for you, and why this industry draws you), you will become more excited and energized about the opportunities. When you discover prospective employers are interested in you, it is a wonderful motivator, and you become much more serious in your career management.

Ask successful executives and leaders of companies, organizations, and institutions about their background and their respective career path to the position they currently hold. You will discover that it is hardly ever a straight line from their start out of college to their current role. You will likely find they entered the job market as most of their peers, and then established themselves through work ethic, passion for excellence, and the ability to make a difference.

Success will come as you treat each opportunity as your dream job. Each position is a building block of experience that you can and will likely draw from as you move forward in your career. Even times where the work is difficult and you feel unappreciated, you will be learning how to manage and lead others, so that when you sense they feel unappreciated, not only can you relate, but you can hopefully make the necessary changes and lead your group to perform at a higher level. It is okay to shoot for the stars, and take risks and challenges, but if you end up in an entry-level role that seems boring and potentially a dead end (even after all your research), connect with other individuals within the organization or company and look for opportunities to build your qualifications to make a move that will not only benefit you, but also the organization and company as well.

DREAMS DON'T WORK UNLESS YOU DO

© Gustavo Frazao/Shutterstock.com

There may be times when your dream job seems like a nightmare. Oftentimes, this happens because you are so focused on the end career destination (manager, director, VP, executive, president, and owner or CEO position) and your frustration shows because you do not want to wait two years or three years to make it to the next level in the organization. Or your frustration also grows because people do not seem to recognize how great you are, and, coincidently, your motivation goes down and you are not willing to put in the time or the effort to truly become credible in your role. You feel like you are not being treated fairly, and because of that, your attitude becomes negative, you become sarcastic as you try to make others aware that you are unhappy, and your enjoyment with the position and the opportunity it may represent eventually withers and dies.

If you want to have a dream job, you do your best to enjoy and make the most out of the adventure that you are in. Start by making a difference, as well as an impact, so that those around you appreciate you and your efforts. If your attitude is right, you will still draw enjoyment from a job well done, even if nobody notices. When you walk through an empty hallway and see a piece of trash, do you pass it by because you did not drop it or because nobody will see you pick it up? With the right attitude, you pick it up regardless of the attention you may/may not get simply because it is the right thing to do.

If you want frustration, added stress, and career roadblocks with your career trajectory, be sure to routinely become upset when others do not see things your way. In addition, you will likewise struggle if you tend to be selfish and are always out for yourself and your own self-interests. You may not realize this, but if this is where you are in your career, others will notice. In addition, coworkers love to talk about the individuals in the office or organization who are like that, and once you are in that "special group," it is hard to remove yourself from it.

One of the things I personally, learned about making each opportunity your dream job is that unless you own the company or everyone works for you, you will have to sell your idea or recommendation when faced with issues mentioned earlier in this chapter. So, do not become frustrated; instead, become creative and communicate with others to find out what they think and why they believe their position is a better option. Remember, maintain the right attitude and, challenging as it may be, even rejoice in your circumstances, and you will become a better and more promotable employee and professional because of the issues you successfully address.

Over the years, we have had numerous students who were at first very uncertain, confused, and stressed about what they were going to do when they graduated. They were so afraid the position they selected would not be what they wanted and they would be stuck in it for the rest of their life. I am not sure where this urban legend began, but that is simply not the way it works.

Those who worry about making the wrong decision tend to not make any decision at all. When we talked with those uncertain, confused, and stressed-out students and helped them realize the potential that they have, the opportunity that is in front of them, and the basic steps to take in order to move forward, their career traction usually improved rather quickly. I have had students who were distraught about their career future, yet in a short amount of time, they were energized and excited. Attitude, as we discussed, plays a large role in this energizing process, and we always see excitement when someone realizes the honest vision of their potential and they begin moving forward towards their career aspirations.

On closing this chapter, I want to share one more story. A quick example: one student was upset, frustrated, and stressed because she was graduating with her undergrad degree in a few months and, from her prospective, had no viable career options. She had been apathetic to her career development and had procrastinated engaging in the career process until she was almost walking down the aisle to graduate. We talked with her about her interests and past experiences, and it became clear that she had an interest in finance and helping others with their business struggles. Financial consulting would be perfect, she felt, and she had done several projects in her academic career that addressed this area. However, she had no direct, professional experience. We targeted the locations she wanted to live and then the firms in those areas that would be exciting to work for. The firms were topflight, elite companies.

The student did her research as we discussed earlier and became a believer that if she prepared to the best of her ability and gave it her best, that was all that she could do. The person met with the firms at a campus career fair and was confident in her research, asked great questions, and showed passion and a strong interest in the firm and industry and ended up being asked to interview with both firms. The student then worked diligently to prepare for the interview (you will learn more about this in chapter eight) and went in confident and energetic. She ultimately received offers from both firms and accepted the offer from her first choice company for her dream job.

What happened to her over the span of a few weeks? How did this go from a train wreck to success? Simple, she had a major attitude change and gained confidence in her ability through her hard work and preparation. She was also not burdened by the stress and anxiety of failure. How can applying to the top firm in the industry be a failure, especially if you prepare and execute properly? How can gaining an opportunity to interview with them and gain incredibly valuable interview experience be a bad thing? How can putting yourself in this position be a negative experience? If she became worried, if she did not have enough experience, or if someone was smarter, and so on, all things out of her current control, she would have not even received a phone interview. She did her research on her interests and how that related to a job; she prepared well and believed in herself because of her efforts. The firm took notice and decided they needed her as part of the company. They offered and she accepted.

You might think this is a onetime story, but it is not. The truth is it is becoming far more regular as students recognize their potential and accept their own personal accountability for success. Students today have so much unharnessed horsepower and so much potential. They just need to be willing to push themselves and realize their potential.

Attitude and your dream job—they go hand in hand throughout your career. One of the most important things you can do to benefit your career is engage fully into the career development process. Do NOT let apathy, procrastination or fear control you.

© Lemau Studio/Shutterstock.com

Chapter 2 Review Questions

1. In the space provided, describe the attitude the book recommends for **YOU** and **your** professional career management? _____

   _____

   _____

   _____

   _____

2. The book speaks to a specific limitation or "one thing" that often prevents an individual from moving forward to realize their career potential. What is that "one thing"?

   a) Education

   b) Money

   c) Talent

   d) Fear

3. According to Chapter 2, the greatest force holding you back from success is?

   a) Your professor

   b) Your parents

   c) You

   d) Your circumstances

4. Describe an event in your life that you can draw strength and determination from?

   _____

   _____

   _____

   _____

   _____

5. What changes would you make to your career development if you had an attitude that everything you did leaves a legacy about who you are? Write a brief statement of what you can do today to take more ownership of your future.

_____

_____

_____

_____

_____

6. How would you act if you knew that the world was recording your actions and those actions and your associated effort would be posted on YouTube each day? What type of attitude would you have? Write down three things that you think people would say about you.

a)

b)

c)

7. What type of attitude should you have in order to secure your dream job?

_____

_____

_____

_____

_____

8. Life can be fun and exciting when you live it without regrets or fear of failure.

a) True

b) False

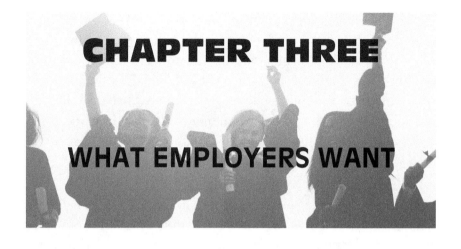

CHAPTER THREE

WHAT EMPLOYERS WANT

Y ou need to fully understand how you will be evaluated when it comes to the recruiting process and your potential employment as an intern or a full-time employee. Your prospective employer is looking to make their company more successful and to do that they want to recruit and hire the highest potential impact player for every open position they have. They want a safe bet with their recruiting dollars as well as the greatest return on their investment (ROI).

This should make perfect sense as you would want the very same thing if you were selecting resources for your team as you prepare to tackle a challenging future project. You would want the best, the brightest, and for most individuals and companies you would also want applicants/individuals that add to and enhance the morale and environment of the office or work space. You would select applicants/individuals who would also fit in culturally with you and your team.

How would you go about evaluating and making selections for your team? If you were able to sit in the recruiter's or hiring manager's seat you may gain some interesting insight into how they value and select talent. The best indicator on future performance would be known or historical performance under similar or forecasted conditions, witnessed by you personally. The next best indicator would be referrals from other teammates or colleagues that you trust and respect regarding their awareness of known or historical performance under similar or forecasted conditions. The third best indicator would be reviewing their background and talking with the applicant/individual about their capabilities and evaluating them through a set of questions and assessments.

The picture that you need to understand is that most college students are under the "third indicator" scenario as they have not performed professionally (full-time work status) in the role they are seeking. Fortunately, for the majority of college students their competition (other college students seeking employment) is under a similar applicant evaluation process. That is why understanding what employers want is so critical. If you think their primary interest is your 4.0 GPA, or your high school activities and heroics, you are mistaken. In addition, by not having a clear understanding of the process, you may have just lost the chance at possibly your top career choice. You may be surprised at not only how you are being evaluated but what the prospective employer believes is important.

Here is a story of a student who struggled taking advantage of the basis of this chapter "What Employers Want." The student was exceptionally bright (3.6 GPA), an active college athlete, and took his college studies seriously. He had a strong resume and as a result had better than average success moving from the applicant status to the interview status with prospective employers. The challenge began when he interviewed. He had potential and should have had multiple offers from various name-brand firms, but he struggled mightily, and for several months failed to receive even one offer, and often did not get a call back or e-mail after the interview. Upon reviewing a series of mock interviews it became clear why he had no success in the interviews. Not only did he not understand "What Employers Want", he genuinely did not care. He was being honest, but from an employer's perspective he had not earned the right to dictate terms to them and act as if he should be their #1 draft choice.

Try as he might, he could not shake the "what's in it for me" attitude. Through practice and several mock interviews he finally realized how his actions, questions, preparation, and personality were being perceived. When he addressed this the interviews became longer, more interesting, and engaging and the offers soon followed. As a new college hire you have to prove yourself and build credibility to earn the right to your first post-college professional role and this continues as you build credibility for promotions and raises.

Here are three articles regarding hiring surveys and insight from respected firms where they speak specifically about hiring college graduates. The first is an article from the National Association for Colleges and Employers (NACE) titled The Attributes Employers Seek on a Candidate's Resume dated December 7, 2016. It states that 70% of the employers reported screening college applicants by GPA and of that group over 60% will use a cutoff of 3.0, which is also the mean and median reported cutoffs for the entire group. The same article describes the following student attributes as being screened by and sought after by employers on a candidate's resume in the following order of priority:

- Ability to work in teams
- Problem solving skills
- Communication skills
- Work ethic
- Leadership
- Initiative
- Analytical skills
- Adaptability
- Detail oriented
- Interpersonal skills
- Technical skills

These attributes were ranked ordered from 78% to 57% of the critical attributes sought by employers according to NACE. The second is an article from TIME, written by Martha C. White, and titled: The Reason College Graduates Can't Get Hired. In the article, there was a survey by the Workforce Solutions Group that said over 60% of the employers said applicants lacked "communication and interpersonal skills" and that a wide margin of managers said today's applicants cannot "think critically and creatively, solve problems or write well." The third is a survey from the premier global staffing firm Adecco supports the above mentioned survey and said "44% of respondents cited soft skills, such as communications, critical thinking and collaboration, as the area with the biggest gap" from the college applicants they reviewed.

These areas are important and you need to credibly demonstrate through your resume and in an interview setting that you are a well-qualified and capable job applicant.

In addition, you can be reasonably certain the following are critically important to prospective employers when it comes to hiring college students and graduates.

*They want someone who brings energy to the workplace

Do you inspire and encourage people you meet or drag them down? You need to find the personal energy, get more sleep, exercise more, eat right, or just smile, but bring energy to every meeting and conversation. There is always a chance that you may get a job because you are the brightest applicant, but it is far more likely that you won't receive a job or internship offer because of the perception that you will be an emotional drain on the organization.

*They want someone that brings a "Can-Do" attitude and has confidence in their capabilities

Do not mistake "Can-Do" for saying "yes" to everything as it is not a blind affirmation to each seemingly meaningless task and experience you are asked about. Employers and their talent recruiting team are looking to evaluate your personality to see if you are a high-maintenance individual that will require a significant amount of energy by management to get you to embrace the company vision or culture. A person with a "Can-Do" attitude "assumes" that there is a greater plan at work than they are aware of and they give others, especially those who are in positions of greater responsibility, the benefit of the doubt and optimistically approach each challenge. There are always many unknowns and unexpected variables and challenges in a business or professional setting and employers want their employees to trust them and to embrace those challenges. Be a person who brings solutions and don't be the person who only points out problems. You have seen people with Can-Do attitudes and you have also seen those without. Picture a sports team where the team is down by a certain number of points or runs with time running out. You can clearly see those that have already embraced defeat compared to those that are optimistically looking for the next opportunity to turn the game around. Those with a "Can-Do" attitude always give their best and every employer is looking for that attribute. As a potential new hire it is important to have this attribute. You may one day become a savvy, respected, and wise veteran of the workforce who has seen enough success and failure to second guess decisions, but wait until you have the experience to go along with the attitude.

*They want a self-starter who is comfortable with minimal direction/supervision

An old coach once said there are two types of people that you never want on your team: those that never do what they are told and those that only do what they are told. A self-starter will look for other tasks when the task they were given is completed and they will assist others when asked to do so. When given a task they will try and learn as much about the task as they can to understand how the task impacts those around them. Do not be the person who has to be given the same instructions multiple times. That says you are not really interested in the role. Do each task that you are given to the best of your ability so that it is an example of your potential.

*They prefer a person with a track record of success

This can be a challenge for a college student who is seeking their first professional role in any chosen industry. You simply have not had the chance/opportunity to develop a track record of success in a professional field. However, recruiters and hiring managers know that past performance often predicts future behavior. You need to understand this because you need performance and result-based bullets to describe your past experiences. In order to be credibly considered ahead of your peers, consider the following scenarios and track your performance:

- When working part-time as a pizza delivery person how would you measure your success and impact to the company?
- When working in your local summer job how would you measure your performance and contribution to the company?
- When working in your first and/or second internship how would you measure the results you brought to the company?

- When you were engaged in athletics, sororities, fraternities, clubs, group projects, intramurals, community activities, and such, was your active presence a contribution to the team's or group's success? Can you measure or identify what you did that made a difference?

It is important to your career development that you think in terms of YOUR contribution to the end result. When others are evaluating you as a potential employee they want to know what type of person you are and if you have made a positive impact on those around you and within organizations or employers you have been affiliated with.

*They prefer a person who is comfortable as a group leader when the need or opportunity presents itself

Being a recognized leader as a new-hire college student means you can identify and quantify your ability or history of moving individuals, groups, and projects to improved performance and or positive impact. You need to recognize the potential to develop these skills when involved in class projects, athletics, fraternity or sorority, club, and other group settings. Once developed and refined they can become important bullet points on your resume to demonstrate credibility as a leader. Leaders are not born they are developed and formed through the challenges and adversities they face. The first step for many college students is stepping up to a position of responsibility in a small group setting. Do not wait for that single large crisis to be a leader, develop those skills in an ongoing manner, through your college career it will serve you well throughout your life, personally and professionally.

*They want someone who is a capable and confident communicator

Communication comes in many forms and you need to be good at all of them. Verbal, written, body language, presentation, and social media all are important communication areas for you.

- Verbally, can you carry on an interesting conversation with an hourly worker and also with a senior executive or professional? You will find if you actively stay on top of important news events in your industry field you will have more to talk about. You will also find that the secret to being a great communicator is being an even better listener. Knowing what your audience is interested in is always beneficial to improving your communication skills. Ask engaging and interesting questions and learn from each meeting.

- Written communication is often taken for granted in a professional setting, yet, if you want to experience a serious roadblock to your career progress communicate as an applicant to an internship or job with misspelled words, improper grammar or worse, communicate in an unprofessional manner. One thing to know and always remember (no matter what industry you select) is that something that is written by pen, pencil or email and text, can become a discoverable item in a legal setting. Do not write it if you would not want to have it read back to you in a court of law. Do not take written communication skills lightly as it is an important part of your career development. Misspelled words on a resume or application or introductory email will kill your chance to make a great first impression.

- Having confident body language will improve your communication ability and impress those who are evaluating you for either hiring or promotion. Good body language is made up of an engaging and energetic personality, firm handshake, good eye contact, professional posture, and dress. An engaging and energetic personality shows you want to be there and that you are interested. A firm handshake and good eye contact shows that you are confident.

- Professional posture means you carry yourself in a confident manner. Some signs that you are not confident would be nervously moving and shifting your feet, slumping your shoulders, slouching, not maintaining good eye contact, rubbing or fidgeting with your hands, and frequently licking or biting your lips. You have seen people walk and carry themselves when they are positive, upbeat, and confident, and you have seen people walk and carry themselves when they seem depressed, beaten down, unsure of themselves, and overly shy.

- Presentation is simply being able to make a point in a room full of people in a confident manner. You should be able to convincingly make your point in multiple settings, from a formal presentation to an informal discussion with a small group. If by chance, you meet with a group in an interview setting be sure and include and engage everyone in the room. When responding to questions and speaking make good eye contact with the person who asked the question and include others in your glances. It is natural to be nervous, but this is your time to speak confidently and if you have prepared appropriately you will do fine. Be sure and introduce yourself when you come into the room and shake hands with each person there. When finished, shake hands again and smile.

- Lastly, social media communicates many things to potential employers and you should be aware that it will be scrutinized. Potential employers regularly review social media sites of applicants looking for areas of concern. One of the things you need to understand about the recruiting process is that most recruiters are looking to narrow down the selection/applicant pool and they make quick decisions to narrow the field. Make sure your social media reflects a balanced and professional presence. We recommend having nothing on your social media that is controversial or questionable. You do not want to give them a reason to move you out of the interview list, so keep your social media site professional.

*They want to make sure you can pass the "airplane test"

This term is used to describe an informal evaluation of your personality, hygiene, and communication skills to see if the group you would be working with would prefer to jump from an airplane as opposed to sitting next to you for 4 hours on a business trip.

*They want someone who clearly shows them that they are truly interested in the opportunity because they have prepared and are informed about the company and the role

You should research the company and its culture and you should make it a point to know its products, strategy, competitors, industry perception, strengths and weaknesses, unique market position, and recent news and trends. You can get most, if not all, of this information off the Internet. If the company is a publicly traded company, there will be a significant amount of information available and you should review its most recent Annual Report, Quarterly Reports, and Earnings Calls. You can find this from the company website. You can also review industry reports and trends.

The more prepared you are, the more confident you will be, and as you can imagine, employers want to hire informed applicants. As an example, when employers come to campus to speak, they often ask if anyone has questions after finishing the presentation. When a student asks a thought-provoking or insightful question, the employer will almost always glance at me as an unspoken code to make sure they get the student's resume or have a chance to meet with the student after the session is complete. They can tell when someone is truly interested. Those students make it to the "I-want-to-interview-you list."

The following is the minimum recommendation for preparation regarding a basic understanding of the *industry*, *company*, and *position* you are seeking. This recommendation is targeted towards a business-degreed student, but it would be relevant to a student from a different academic area by inserting the critical knowledge components from the associated industry, company, and position or role.

THINGS you should know about the INDUSTRY that you are interested in

- ➤ Research the forecasts and trends of the revenue and profitability of the industry
- ➤ Research the number of major players and their associated market share
- ➤ Research expert opinions on the future outlook of the industry (Wall Street, Bloomberg, Industry Associations)
- ➤ Look at the major threats and opportunities to the industry
- ➤ Look at the industry with regard to its global footprint
- ➤ Research major industry associations for recent issues and events
- ➤ Review the companies that are considered innovators in this industry
- ➤ Look at the Merger and Acquisition (M&A) activity over past 3 years within the industry

THINGS you should know about the COMPANY you are interested in

- ➤ Look at the company's annual report (if a public company) and other published financial documents to gain a sense as to the future potential and forecasts of the company
- ➤ Research the company regarding the annual revenue dollars ($), the employee headcount, major locations, primary business units, senior leadership, and company culture
- ➤ Check the last 3 years of stock activity (if a public company)
- ➤ Read the last year of major press releases from the website

> Review the company's major competitors and their market share (this will be visible in their annual report if it is a public company)

> Understand the part that globalization plays in this company

> Understand the company's top customers and the percentage (%) of business they provide to the company

> Understand the company's major products or services, and their associated strategy and performance if published

> Know the stated strategic mission and core values of the company (these will often be on the company's website and or in their annual report)

> Look at the legal and Merger and Acquisition (M&A) activity at this company in the last 3–5 years

THINGS you should know about the POSITION or ROLE you are seeking

> Understand the primary requirements and qualification of the position and be able to speak to how you are qualified for each, then review your resume to insure it shows a strong fit for these requirements

> Reach out to friends, family, professors, career management personnel, and alumni who can help you connect to individuals who have worked at the company or in the department or have during their professional career held the same or similar role. You can do this via LinkedIn or through the above-mentioned contacts

> Research through the above bullet how your performance in this role would be evaluated

> Review the position via www.glassdoor.com where you can review the company and position as well as their interview process

➤ Uncover the salary norms for this type of position (inside and outside of this company); www.glassdoor.com is an excellent resource for reviewing salaries for this type of position

➤ Understand what location you would be working from and the cost of living issues associated with that location

*Employers want smart, bright, and intelligent new hires

Often internship and job postings for college applicants contain a minimum grade point average (GPA) requirement. For most postings, this is 3.0 out of a 4.0 scale. Some of the more elite positions require a 3.25 or 3.5 GPA. The GPA minimum is not a 100% deal-killer on every opportunity, but it can be a tiebreaker to see if you will be contacted for an interview, especially with many applicants seeking the position. You should know that not meeting the GPA minimum in a position that is an online posting might well cause your application to not be considered. Some employers take into account athletic or extracurricular activities, but most do not, especially within their scanning systems. So, do the best you can to stay at or above the 3.0 GPA minimum.

There is another segment that falls under the section of "What Employers Want." This is an area that is gaining more and more traction in the recruiting industry as employers endeavor to improve the odds that they are only focusing on the "best candidates." This segment is employer administered personality and assessment tests so that they can increase the return on their hiring investment (ROI as mentioned earlier in this chapter).

Employers hope that by using personality and assessment tests to pre-qualify those applicants that they are considering for an interview, it will narrow the amount of unqualified applicants they bring into the interview process. This will save the firm time and money. The employer hopes by using these personality and assessment tests that they can accomplish two things. They will limit those that appear qualified but, in fact are not based on the test scores compared to behavioral role ratings. In addition, these tests will enhance the likelihood they will recruit someone who has similar attributes and characteristics to others who have worked in like roles and have had success and made positive contributions previously to the firm. These tests can measure a wide array of skills, characteristics, and attributes. The tests can also measure the applicant's fit compared to characteristics from a large database of successful professionals who have had success in a similar role.

The applicant is given an extensive series of questions that rank them against known characteristics which are critical for the role they are applying for. The applicant is then scored against the ranking required by the employer and those that fit within the band of the ranking are called in for an interview and those that do not are not. These tests are sophisticated and there is not a secret formula guaranteed to fool the tests and secure a position that you are likely not a fit for. You should get a good night's sleep before the test and answer consistently with the first correct answer that comes to mind, don't try and game the test. If you have done your homework on the role that you feel qualified for and are passionate about, and you are as clear as you can be about the requirements and qualifications of the role, you will do fine. You can prepare however, if the test is a skills-based test as there are likely sample tests available on the Internet. While they will probably be different from the actual test you will take, you will at least gain experience in the testing process.

Just know that this type of testing is increasing and if you were the employer and you were putting your company dollars into recruiting for a position, you would want to do your very best to insure the person you hire has the highest probability for success.

Many of the things you have read in this chapter may seem like common sense, and basic attributes for hiring good candidates . . . and they are. What is not as commonplace is the fact that students often do not recognize soon enough the need for more personal accountability with their career management. You have to work diligently to create a body of work that encourages the employer to want to interview you. You also want this same body of work to place you at the top of the interview list versus your peers and, ultimately, results in an exciting internship or job offer.

In Chapter 4, Resume, we will address how to develop your resume to show a high-level fit for the position you are qualified and passionate about. In Chapter 7, Connecting and Communicating, we will show you how to identify and connect with individuals who can assist you in evaluating the critical requirements for the position as well as the culture and structure within the employer application and interview process. In Chapter 8, Interviewing, we will show you how to prepare for and succeed in the interview.

It is very important that you clearly understand and appreciate "What Employers Want" and that you actively demonstrate credibility in the areas that are most important to the employer. You must sell yourself, your brand, and your potential impact to the employer. As a new college graduate with zero to minimal actual professional work experience, it is not about your needs and wants as much as it is about the prospective employer's needs and wants.

© Bacho/Shutterstock.com

Chapter 3 Review Questions

1. List four characteristics that employers are looking for in a new employee?

   _____

   _____

   _____

   _____

2. How can your attitude address some of the characteristics an employer is seeking?

   _____

   _____

   _____

3. What is the "airplane test" and how can you insure that you can pass it with flying colors?

   a) What is it? _____

   b) How can you insure that you will pass the "airplane test"? _____

   _____

   _____

   _____

4. There are three major questions you need to be able to answer convincingly for a recruiter. Fill in the blanks to show you understand the three questions:

   a) Why are you interested in this _____?

   b) What is it about this _____
      that excites and interests you?

   c) Why is this _____
      a great fit for you?

5. Picture your ideal job (company, industry, and role).
   Answer each of the three questions in writing so that a
   recruiter would clearly know you have researched and are
   truly interested in the company and industry . . . and that
   you are clearly qualified to make a positive impact in the
   role/opportunity you seek.

   a) Why this company?

   _____

   _____

   _____

   _____

   b) Why this industry?

   _____

   _____

   _____

   _____

   c) Why do you think you are the best fit for this role?

   _____

   _____

   _____

   _____

6. What do you think are the most important characteristics
   and abilities a person must possess to be successful in the
   role that you are most interested in? How do you rate
   yourself in those areas on a scale of 1–10, with 1 being
   absolutely no chance for success and 10 being incredibly
   qualified? _____

   _____

   _____

CHAPTER FOUR

RESUME

Y ou want a resume that rewards you with an interview. As we discussed in Chapter One, the resume is NOT a chronological or biographical sketch of your life. It is NOT a list of tasks you have performed and written like a job description, NOR is it focused on areas that are insignificant and not relevant to your audience (recruiting personnel and hiring managers). Your resume must be results and performance based and show a clear fit to the opportunity you are seeking.

Typically, an undergraduate or graduate student with two years or less work experience would have a one-page resume. A professional or graduate student with more than five years work experience would likely have a two page resume. Students in other fields such as education, healthcare, and other non-business areas would have resumes with various modifications based upon specific industry guidelines. It is generally ok to go over one page as long as you have something noteworthy to say, and if it further qualifies you as a good fit for the opportunity you are seeking; but normally one-page resumes are standard. Remember this is not a novel about you. The resume should be a brief summary of your background, experiences, and skills which are relevant to the position you desire. The **primary purpose** of your resume is to gain an interview.

Before we dive headstrong into resumes, let's first discuss the types of personal attributes you should be highlighting on a resume. Many of the jobs you apply to in your career may not be something you already have direct experience doing. Because of this reality, employers are looking for candidates who have demonstrated something called ***transferable skills***. Transferable skills are soft and hard skills you have acquired in other settings that you more than likely would exhibit in future employment settings. These transferable skills are broken down into four main categories: Interpersonal Skills, Organization Skills, Leadership Skills, and Communication Skills. Below you will find a partial listing of transferable skills broken down into these four main categories.

Interpersonal Skills

- Relating well with others
- Responding to concerns
- Motivating people
- Assisting others
- Resolving conflicts
- Being a team player

Organization Skills

- Follow-through
- Multitasking
- Setting and attaining goals
- Meeting deadlines
- Planning
- Time management

Leadership Skills

- Decision-making
- Evaluating
- Managing
- Planning
- Supervising
- Delegating
- Initiating
- Motivating others
- Problem-solving
- Team-building

Communication Skills

- Advising
- Explaining
- Persuading or selling
- Public speaking
- Writing and editing
- Translating
- Articulating
- Instructing
- Presenting
- Training

When compiling information for your resume, you want to focus on finding ways to showcase these transferable skills from your prior job,internship, organization leadership roles, or class project experiences.

Let's review some basic formatting guidelines so that your resume has the greatest chance of making it through a company's resume filter. Most sophisticated companies use a resume scanning system that looks for keywords or a base filtering system called applicant tracking system or ATS. These systems scan for keywords and are able to do what it would take hundreds of human resources or talent coordinators to do. Major companies receive thousands of applications and resumes for entry-level college graduate opportunities. There is no way the initial volume of applications and resumes can be efficiently reviewed by a recruiting group. Instead, they use a filtering system to select resumes based upon key word hits and meeting a preestablished quantity of qualifications. On this fact alone, you can see the importance of showing a solid fit with your resume. However, what you may not know is the format you use or the way you save the file that contains your resume could have significant bearing on whether your resume makes it through this initial review.

Here are some guidelines that will help your resume from becoming "flagged" unnecessarily due to the screening of ATS:

- The safest format for your resume is Microsoft™ Word format, and if you cannot save in Word such as .doc or .docx, save the resume as "Text." However, when you use Word, do not build your resume using tables. Simply use the enter/return, space, or tab function to build your resume.

- Do not save your resume as HTML, PDF, WordPerfect, or RTF unless required to do so to complete the application process. Many systems want PDF and if that is required then you should provide your resume in that specific format. We would highly encourage you however, to provide your resume in Word format if that is allowable.

- Use plain black font on a white template and standard webrecognized fonts such as Calibri, Times New Roman or Arial.

- Do not use document headers or footers as some resume software systems cannot read these. Most Applicant Tracking Systems are designed to start reading from the first line in the document, not the header or footer. If you insert your name and contact information in the header the ATS will not be able to parse your data successfully.

- Keep the format simple and avoid graphics, pictures, logos, and fancy templates.

- Do not abbreviate.

- Even after your resume makes it through an ATS, a recruiter or hiring manager may only spend seconds glancing over it. You must clearly show a fit to the position and be brief and to the point in your statements.

A few additional quick points:

- Only bold those items that you truly want to emphasize.

- We read left to right, so place the most important items on the left. This is why it is recommended to place dates and locations toward the right-hand side of the page and employers' names, job titles, and performance bullets on the left.

- Spend at least as much time reviewing the job/internship opportunity you are seeking as you do preparing your resume. If you don't understand the requirements, you will not have much success showing a strong fit in your resume.

- USE SPELL CHECK. Do not send a resume that has not been checked multiple times. You only get one chance to make a first impression.

- Send your finished resume to a mentor, professor, friend, or connection so they can review the resume for grammar, content, and spelling. Always have a second and or a third person take a look at your finished version.

The following is a recommended resume template. The example template provides tips and hints as to when to include something, when not to include something and how to set up your resume. The tips and hints are listed in brackets ([ ]) for your benefit. The recommendations include instructions about format, style, content and fit with respect to connecting your capabilities to the qualifications and requirements of the position for which you are applying.

This resume has been tested for readability with several ATS systems along with career tools such as Jobscan and VMOCK.

These tools are designed to improve your overall resume and increase your ATS score and help you land that interview.

Having a resume that is readable by ATS systems is the first step to success. If the system cannot read your resume they can't score you. If they cannot score you-you are not a candidate. This template will result in 100 percent readability.

RESUME TEMPLATE

Your Name

Street Address · City, State. Zip

Phone Number · Email Address

www.linkedin.com/in/yourname

CAREER PROFILE

This is a professional summary of you written in 3rd person. This brief 3-5 sentence shows a strong fit to the position you are applying for, and highlight your most desirable attributes. This section should showcase your personal brand and your deliverables to the company. Remember to support your qualifications in your experiences referenced below.

EDUCATION

College Attended–City, State

Graduation Date

Degree

- Major; GPA (Omit if less than 3.00)
- [Academic organizations or student leadership experiences]
- [Case competitions and Major relevant projects]
- [Study Abroad experiences]

EXPERIENCE

ORGANIZATION

Month Year – Month Year

[Optional – Company descriptors are in italics to describe unfamiliar companies, Keep to 1 Line]

Position Title

- [Open resume bullet points with a variety of action verbs to avoid repetition]
- [Include details that are performance oriented and quantify results when possible]
- [Avoid resume bullets with "hanging words" – Single words on the 2nd line. Use resume space wisely and make sure resume is weighted properly]
- [Use Calibri font. Font sizes – Section Heading 14, Name 17, Spacer lines: 8-6, Text 11-10.5]

ORGANIZATION

Month Year – Month Year

Position Title

- [Showcase your transferable skills (i.e. Interpersonal Skills, Organization Skills, Leadership Skills, Communication Skills]
- [Experience Bullets need to be performance based. Focus on deliverables - not tasks or things]
- [Focus on how you added value; demonstrate what you accomplished; exhibit the impact you made]

ORGANIZATION

Month Year – Month Year

Position Title

- [Internships dates can be denoted by season and year; i.e. Summer XXXX]
- [Avoid having one bullet point, minimum of two per heading]
- [Leadership roles, volunteer work, class projects, etc. can be added as experiences if relevant]

ADDITIONAL

- [Noteworthy awards and/or accomplishments]
- [List foreign languages and your skill level (include Native, Fluent, or Conversational)]
- [Technical Skills – Be specific. Do not just list Microsoft Office suite skills]
- [Leadership activities, volunteer work, and/or unique interests]

Now let's review each of the sections on the resume.

Contact Information

The section for your name and contact information is fairly straightforward, but just be aware that it is unlikely you will receive a call for an interview if your e-mail address is something unprofessional. It is best to use your university e-mail address if possible. In regards to your mailing address it is acceptable to use your college address. However, if you are from Massachusetts and you are going to college in Texas and you are seeking an internship in Boston, consider using your home address. Additionally, your voicemail message should be professional. You will have calls from recruiters, and you want your first impression to be a professional one.

Career Profile

The next section is titled "Career Profile." Some people prefer to title this section "Summary" or "Profile." This section is one of the most important tools you can use to gain the interest of the recruiter or hiring manager.

Recruiters prefer and greatly appreciate the "Career Profile" section as it gives them a very quick overview of the candidate and sums up their qualifications and fit for the role. Otherwise, they have to search all over the resume for this and, very often, they will just quit reading and go on to another resume. Look at this section as your mini-elevator speech or personal brand statement.

The "Career Profile" should show why you are the strongest fit for the role, and it should also highlight your most desirable, employable attributes. You have between three to five lines to represent your personal brand and show a strong fit for the requirements of the opportunity. The "Career Profile" does this well by highlighting and showcasing your personal brand and, hopefully, convinces the recruiter or hiring manager that you are someone that they definitely should interview.

Your "Career Profile" should be written in third person; be concise and specific about what makes you uniquely qualified for the opportunity. Do not overuse statements that overstate your credibility. If you have zero experience, but you portray yourself as a CEO or senior executive in waiting, they won't take the rest of the resume seriously.

Remember to highlight not only your hard skills, but also discuss critical soft skills. Recruiters are looking for a great mixture of both hard and soft skills. Today, soft skills are just as valuable as hard skills. Don't be afraid to mix in both skill sets in the Career Profile.

Here are a few examples of Career Profiles to help you with the concept. These would be appropriate examples for a business school student (undergraduate and graduate):

© ibreakstock/Shutterstock.com

FINANCE

Driven **Finance/Business Analyst** candidate with experience in excel modeling, financial statement review, and business analytics. Keen ability to take financials and develop big-picture strategy that has lasting impact on core business decisions. Strong work ethic with ability to travel or relocate.

Investment Banking Associate with five years' experience in multinational financial institutions. Skilled at financial modeling and quantitative analysis. Able to summarize sizable and complex amounts of financial data, and make effective decisions in the context of time-sensitive projects. **Certified Treasury Professional, Charted Financial Analyst Level I**

MARKETING

Marketing candidate with experience developing and executing strategic marketing campaigns for innovative start-up firms. Passion for enhancing product brand potential and supporting recommendations with research and solid analytics. Skilled at selling new ideas and taking projects in new directions while creating buy-in from all parties. Skilled at aligning vendor ideas and capabilities with client needs.

Marketing Manager with six-plus years of consistent success in global marketing. Proven manager with strengths in business analysis, brand development, and product management. Excellent cross-functional team-building skills, with a true passion for building marketing teams from the ground up. Recognized by management for exceeding profitability, productivity, and marketing benchmarks.

SALES/BUSINESS DEVELOPMENT

Business Development and Client Relations Coordinator with experience in retail sales, marketing, and client development roles. Analytical thinker with a proven track record for surpassing performance objectives, leading by example, and building cohesiveness and unity among team members.

Sales Manager with four years' experience across a variety of marketing and business development projects. Driven individual with a proven track record of taking product lines in decline and crisis to a place of sustainable growth. Excellent ability to drive initiatives through big-picture vision casting, effective deployment of resources, and dynamic presentations.

OPERATIONS

Supply Chain Analyst candidate with experience in leading projects, creating corrective action plans, and managing cultural differences. Strong understanding of supply chain issues, problem-solving measures, and applying analytic metrics to supply chain challenges. Excellent communicator skilled at vendor negotiations.

Operations Management candidate with five years of professional experience in project management. Recognized by management and peers as a strong critical thinker and team leader who can drive projects to peak performance. Skilled in resource allocation and budgeting and government contract negotiations.

INFORMATION TECHNOLOGY

IT Management Candidate who excels under challenging and high-stress environments and consistently meets project deadlines. Diverse professional experience in handling client technical calls and supporting customer relationships. Excellent ability to communicate technical ideas to nontechnical users.

IT Project Consultant with six years' experience leading projects, supervising staff, and managing budgets for multinational, global organizations. Recognized for efficiently leading large technology teams of engineers, analysts, and professional support staff. Successful IT consulting experience with Fortune 500 clients.

A Career Profile is only as good as the content. As a college student, a new college grad, or experienced professional you need to be able to show recruiters you are the right person for the job. The Career Profile is the easiest and most efficient way to increase you ATS scores. Here are a few suggestions on how to customize your Career Profile based on your specific need.

In these examples, you can see the modifications have been made under the career profile section. The focus becomes on those specific skills that you have that best meet the requirements of the job. The career profile section is a critical place to show fit. Show the recruiter that you can do the job and you can get results. The "Career Profile" examples below should be used when recruiters are seeking specific technical or engineering skills. Make sure when you add content to the template that you don't violate any of the previously discussed ATS rules. Please make sure the formatting is simple and you only use the space and tab keys to set up additional content.

TECHNICAL

Patty M. Neff

One Bear Place #97096 · Waco, TX. 76798

www.linkedin.com/in/pattyneff

(254) 710-3555 · patty_neff@baylor.edu

CAREER PROFILE

IT management candidate with a track record of consistently meeting project deadlines under challenging and stressful environments. Diverse professional experience in handling customer relationships and IT support. Excellent ability to communicate technical ideas to non-technical users. *Technical skills include:*

Version Control:	VSS, Serena Dimensions	**Web Technologies:**	JSP, Servlets, JavaScript, HTML, XML
Proprietary Software:	Vignette Content Management 7.3.0.5, FAST ESP 5.0.4	**Java Technologies:**	2EE, JAVA, JDBC
		Databases:	IBM DB2 9 Certified Associate
Operating systems:	UNIX, Windows XP, Windows Vista	**Application Servers:**	Web Sphere Application Server 5.1, IRAD 6.0

ENGINEERING

Patty M. Neff   One Bear Place #97096 · Waco, TX. 76798
www.linkedin.com/in/pattyneff   **(254) 710-3555 · patty_neff@baylor.edu**

CAREER PROFILE

Mechanical Engineering candidate experienced in engineering analysis, kinematics and kinetics of particles and rigid bodies, and Thermodynamics. Strong analytical mind with the ability to solve complex problems. Proven leader with project background in machine design, fluid mechanics, and electrical networks and systems. Strong foundation in math with a track record of consistently meeting project deadlines under challenging and stressful environments.

Engineering Proficiencies:

Mechanical Design	Manufacturing Process Control	Solid Modeling
Robotics	Design Graphics	AutoCAD
C and C++	MATLAB	Assembly

These templates provide examples on how you can customize the Career Profile and other sections to fit for your specific industry, function, and experience level. These tips will help you create a career profile that clearly shows fit to the position you are applying for and allow the ATS system to give you the score you need to possibly land a first round interview.

Education

This section is typically located after the Career Profile section for an undergrad student as it is the most recognized asset the student could bring to an organization. List your most recent education first. I would recommend using the format provided in the templates on the previous pages as this has been well received by recruiters. Be sure and spell out your degree and do not abbreviate. Also list your GPA if it is 3.00 or greater. List your concentration such as Marketing, Economics, International Studies, Chemistry, etc. It is also acceptable to list your major projects and awards, for example, if you received first place in a case competition or business plan competition. Anything that shows excellence when compared to your peers or in a competitive setting would be worthwhile. In general, high school education is not something that we recommend adding to your resume.

However, we do recommend adding your SAT, ACT and class rank if it clearly shows your performance above your peers. In addition, if you are interested in a career in the consulting industry you will likely be asked to provide that information in the application process.

If you are an inexperienced master's student you will use the same advice above. If you are more experienced you may adjust your template to move the Education section down towards the end of the page. If your brand is a newly minted graduate student and you are using that to land a job then your education section would be under the Career Profile section.

If you are an experienced graduate or professional and you are relying not only on your education but a successful work history you would reposition your Education section towards the end of your resume so you could showcase the Experience section of your resume. Remember the resume is real estate. We want to highlight what best makes you the ideal candidate for the position. So use the real estate of the page or pages to your advantage.

Some students may be graduate students or dual degree students. Below are recommendations on how to adjust your template to reflect these scenarios.

DUAL DEGREE STUDENT

EDUCATION
YOUR UNIVERSITY, Hankamer School of Business – City, State   December 2019
Master of Business Administration Dual Degree Program **(GPA 3.93)**
Master of Science and Information Systems, Dual Degree Program
- Concentration in Finance; GPA 3.6 [Omit if less than 3.0] GMAT 710 [Omit if lower than 650]
- Student leadership bullets in this section only

GRADUATE STUDENT

EDUCATION

YOUR UNIVERSITY, Hankamer School of Business – City, State   December 2019
Master of Business Administration Dual Degree Program **(GPA 3.93)**
Master of Science and Information Systems, Dual Degree Program
  • Concentration in Finance; GPA 3.6 [Omit if less than 3.0] GMAT 710 [Omit if lower than 650]
  • Student leadership bullets in this section only
YOUR UNIVERSITY, Hankamer School of Business - City, State   May 2012
Bachelor of Technology (GPA 3.75)
  • Major: Networking and Wireless Technologies
  • Undergraduate Bullet Points are optional

Experience

The Experience section is critical and will be heavily scrutinized for fit and potential benefit to the company that is considering interviewing you.

If you have experience with a noteworthy or widely recognized company, there is no need to provide a one-line description. If it is a smaller firm, then it would be beneficial to describe it so the person reviewing your resume can evaluate your responsibility within that role.

The most important aspect of your Experience section is the performance bullets. These are NOT a description of your job duties or a statement of how you spent your time. Instead, these are highlights of what you did to make a difference at the company. If you are thinking, "I don't think I did anything special," then now is the time to look at how you apply yourself to your work and the overall difference you make in the organization by being on their payroll.

Think of each performance bullet as being results based. A way to picture or better understand this process is to think of a football player in a program you receive as you enter a football game. If all you had is a picture of the person in uniform, then all you know is the person is on the football team. You have no idea if this person is a strong contributor to the team's success or if he just dresses out each week and stands on the sidelines. However, if you see the personal results and statistics as well as comparison to other players and rankings, you then have a much better picture of the person's impact on the team. Your performance bullets fulfill the same function on your resume. It is important that you are able to show you are a person who contributes to the success of the organization and that the manner you contribute is a direct connection to the role you are seeking. Not many companies want a person that is going to just stand on the sidelines. If you find yourself standing more than contributing, then make a decision and, a commitment, to put more energy into your opportunities.

Your bullets should begin with action verbs such as led, created, developed, increased, supervised, managed, analyzed, etc.

Include at least two performance bullets for even a three-month internship experience. If it is six months to a year, then include more than two, hopefully more performance bullets. Think in terms of results and how your resume should clearly show this. Have enough meaningful, result-oriented bullet points to clearly show a strong fit for the role you are seeking.

Experience Bullet Point Examples

Weak Bullet Point Examples (BEFORE)

- Reviewed company financial statements
- Waited tables and served customers
- Created a company training manual
- Filed papers for real estate department

Improved Bullet Point Examples (AFTER):

- Analyzed financial statements of 50+ companies with over $25M in outstanding loans, reconciled financial reporting errors and maintained FDIC regulatory compliance
- Increased revenues and strengthened customer retention by delivering exceptional guest service to an average of 80 clients daily, leading team with over $60,000 in monthly sales

- Designed and delivered a 215-page company training manual, on time and within budget, decreasing training time and improving performance by 20%
- Organized 3,000+ documents & increased the real estate department's productivity by 15%

If you are a student or someone who is short on work experience you should add content that helps you show the recruiter that given the chance you can do the job well. You should consider adding content from your classes that would allow the recruiters to see how you are going to perform. This could be in the form of a Capstone or Consulting project, Fraternity/Sorority leadership experience, or a Case Competition Team. Any content that you can add to show how you performed in a work or project setting is critical. Here are some examples below.

CLASS PROJECTS

EXPERIENCE

YOUR UNIVERSITY, Hankamer School of Business – City, State   Fall 20XX
Investment Portfolio Analyst – Portfolio Management Practicum
- Co-led Oil and Gas Sector Analyst Team for Portfolio Practicum class valued at over $2,000,000 dollars
- Researched, analyzed, and provided recommendations on portfolio adjustments to oil and gas sector stocks resulting in a 6% value increase

*Please use the semester and year format. (Summer 20XX / Fall 20XX / Spring 20XX)

CONSULTING PROJECTS

EXPERIENCE

COMPANY – City, State   Fall 20XX
Your University Consultant Project – Focus Firm Class
- Identified and presented $4,200,000 NPV pilot program to executive management on e-commerce opportunities in domestic emerging markets resulting in a test market product launch
- Researched, analyzed, and created financial models to evaluate e-commerce trends and opportunities in the food and beverage industry by analyzing market potential, share, and new product viability

*Please use the semester and year format. (Summer 20XX / Fall 20XX / Spring 20XX)

STUDENT ORGANIZATIONS

EXPERIENCE

STUDENT ORGANIZATION, YOUR UNIVERSITY – City, State   **Fall 20XX**
Position Title

- Created and launched on campus multi-channel marketing campaign focused on increasing membership resulting in the addition of 40 new members
- Developed financial models and Excel reports to manage and direct the organizations $500,000 plus dollar operating budget and provide accurate reporting to the national organization

*Please use the semester and year format. (Summer 20XX / Fall 20XX / Spring 20XX)

Additional

This section can be called many things depending on what you need to add to your resume to show a strong fit for the opportunity. Only add those things that are relevant and significant to your intended audience. You might title this section Community Service, Leadership, Additional Qualifications, or Accomplishments and Awards. If you have additional items that will enhance your qualification for the position you are seeking, be sure and list them. Just be sure, they are relevant and noteworthy.

Resume Template

We have given you a completed resume example below. This will help you see what your finished product should look like. This template does not provide formatting advice, but actual content that may help you create a polished resume for yourself. Please make sure you create your own original content when you create your resume.

Patty M. Neff

One Bear Place #97096 · Waco, TX. 76798
(254) 710-3555 · patty_neff@baylor.edu

www.linkedin.com/in/pattyneff

CAREER PROFILE

Bilingual Finance candidate experienced in excel modeling, financial statement review, and market evaluation. Strong communicator that makes decisions quickly and accurately. Analytical thinker with a proven track record for exceeding expectations, leading by example, and delivering projects on time. Results driven individual that thrives in a collaborative fast paced environment.

EDUCATION

BAYLOR UNIVERSITY–Waco, Texas   **May 2020**

Bachelor of Business Administration

- **Majors**: Finance; Management Information Systems
- **Overall GPA**: 3.75; **Major GPA**: 3.83
- **Dean's Academic Honor List**: Fall 2016, Spring 2017, Fall 2017, Spring 2018, Fall 2018

EXPERIENCE

Deloitte & Touche LLP–Dallas, Texas   **May 2018-August 2018**

Analyst Intern

- Developed planning procedures and financial statements to help prepare for an upcoming audit
- Collaborated in cross-functional project and presented information to 4 Executive Strategy and Business Development representatives
- Prepared over 800 invoices for refund claims resulting in client savings of more than $400,000 in taxes

Alpha Delta Pi Sorority–Waco, Texas   **January 2018 – Present**

Executive Recruitment Chair

- Recruited 30 members doubling the size of the organization since residing in this position
- Led 6 seminars over the course of a semester to develop members level of professionalism
- Utilized Excel to manage a $25,000 budget, and raised over $5,000 to be donated to philanthropy

TEXAS Roadhouse–Waco Texas   **June 2017-December 2017**

Hostess

- Increased sales by 15% by promoting weekly specials verbally and by social media
- Strategized and prepared table logistics for large parties to ensure successful service
- Managed 75-100 customers and 8 waiters at a time during peak hours, leading the Team in efficiency

ADDITIONAL

- **Computer Skills**: Visual Basics, SQL, SAP, QuickBooks, Excel, PowerPoint
- **Foreign Languages**: Native Spanish speaker – Fluent written and verbal skills
- **Organizations**: Baylor Women in Business, Alpha Delta Pi Sorority
- **Activities**: Intramural Sports, Competed in Accenture IT Intervention Competition, Participated in Marketing Project with Dell

ATS

Applicant Tracking Systems are beneficial to recruiters because they automate the process. They make the arduous task of viewing thousands of resumes into a workable number. Review the following link to look at how Applicant Tracking Systems work.

https://www.jobscan.co/applicant-tracking-systems

This system will scan your resume against all other applicants during this process and rank you compared to the job description and the search requested by the recruiter. Your goal is to maximize your score and present your best foot forward compared to the job description. The higher the score the better chance you have of landing the first-round interview. If your resume is unreadable the system doesn't try and fix it for you. The system deletes it automatically. Research we found says almost 70 percent of all resumes submitted through ATS are unreadable and those are not considered viable candidates to fill those positions. No actual recruiter will view your resume. Those resumes go to the virtual round file, the trash. The candidates who chose to use a readable resume will have a chance to interview. The candidates that chose to not only use a readable template but spend the time to "FIT" resume will be rewarded with higher ATS scores and therefore will receive more first-round interviews.

Resume Fitting Process

Because most companies use Applicant Tracking Systems we need to make sure not only the template is readable from our previous discussions, but we also need to make sure we "FIT" our resume to the job description. This is the most critical piece in the application process - Fitting your resume to the job. This is the process of taking a job description and analyzing it for keywords and phrases that can be used ethically in your resume to establish yourself as an ideal candidate for the positions. This process is trying to increase your ATS score.

This process can seem cumbersome to most applicants, but it's recommended that you go through the FIT process every time you apply for a position. To most applicants, this seems to be a waste of time, but fitting is critical to increasing ATS scores which results in more first-round interviews. If you continue to send out a basic non-fitted resume your traction to firstround interviews will be very low, usually less than five percent. Remember if you think you are a true fit for a position and you keep applying to those positions with little to no activity something is wrong. Usually, it's because the applicant didn't take the time to fit their resume. A readable, fitted resume should get at least 25 to 35 percent traction to land first round interviews.

We can accomplish this several ways. Let's explore a lowtech option first. This process is as simple as printing out the job description and highlighting and identifying the following items:

- Essential skills, critical success factors, job functions
- Roles and responsibilities
- Technical skillsets, required core competencies
- Specific keywords and phrases used in the job description
- Identify words used the most

All critical information needed to be successful

Once this process is complete we need to verify this information was included on the resume used to apply for this specific job. If not, we need to add these specifics to increase our ATS score. Think about using keywords multiple times. Use the same language and phrases used by the employer in the job description. If they use the words Excel then use that terminology. If they prefer to call it Excel modeling or other skills then you need to "FIT" your resume and use the same exact words, language, and phrasing the employer uses. This will drastically increase your ATS score and help you land that first round interview. In today's ATS filled recruiting world, you must "PLAY THE GAME". Meaning the "FITTING" process must be done to increase your score against your competition applying for the job you want.

Throughout this process, you may find a significant disconnect between what is on your resume versus what you think you are representing. Unless you are using the same keywords, phrases, skills, and language they will not see you as you see yourself. Take the time to "FIT" your resume every time. It's a full-time job to find a full-time job so put in the work. Remember computers are ranking data and scoring the information you provide, they are not able to make inferences human recruiters will make. They simply search and find the best applicants resume that fits the job description, so be exact. Help the system read your resume.

Low tech works, but Jobscan provides a robust tool at an affordable price for job applicants to help navigate the waters of ATS. Jobscan is a premium service offered at www.jobscan.co that allows you to do a pre-application ATS score verification. You simply copy and paste or download your resume into the system. You repeat the same.

© Jobscan. Reprinted by permission.

Action Verb List

Financial	Technical	Operations	Marketing	HR/Training	Communication	Achievement	Management
Acquired	Adapted	Accelerated	Analyzed	Advised	Adapted	Accelerated	Administered
Adjusted	Adjusted	Arranged	Authored	Arranged	Addressed	Accomplished	Analyzed
Administered	Analyzed	Assembled	Broadened	Benchmarked	Advised	Achieved	Approved
Allocated	Applied	Assessed	Captured	Clarified	Affected	Acquired	Arbitrated
Analyzed	Assembled	Catalogued	Changed	Coached	Aided	Activated	Assigned
Appraised	Built	Centralized	Collected	Collaborated	Clarified	Arranged	Briefed
Assessed	Collected	Classified	Composed	Consulted	Coached	Attained	Chaired
Audited	Compiled	Collected	Conceived	Counseled	Communicated	Awarded	Constructed
Augmented	Computed	Compiled	Conceptualized	Educated	Composed	Completed	Contracted
Balanced	Constructed	Coordinated	Conducted	Energized	Coordinated	Coordinated	Coordinated
Budgeted	Designed	Dispatched	Constructed	Enlisted	Delivered	Decreased	Critiqued
Calculated	Developed	Distributed	Created	Explained	Developed	Displayed	Decided
Compiled	Devised	Eliminated	Customized	Facilitated	Directed	Drove	Decreased
Consolidated	Diagnosed	Evaluated	Designed	Familiarized	Educated	Earned	Delegated
Contracted	Discovered	Executed	Developed	Guided	Enabled	Effected	Determined
Controlled	Documented	Expedited	Devised	Hired	Encouraged	Elicited	Developed
Corrected	Engineered	Fabricated	Discovered	Implemented	Evaluated	Executed	Directed
Decreased	Evaluated	Generated	Drafted	Instructed	Explained	Expanded	Energized
Developed	Examined	Implemented	Edited	Interviewed	Facilitated	Expedited	Enforced
Effected	Executed	Inspected	Energized	Investigated	Guided	Experienced	Evaluated
Enhanced	Extracted	Integrated	Enriched	Led	Illustrated	Generated	Formalized
Estimated	Familiarized	Maintained	Established	Mediated	Informed	Improved	Formed
Forecasted	Gathered	Manufactured	Evaluated	Mentored	Instructed	Increased	Founded
Fulfilled	Generated	Merchandised	Forecasted	Merged	Interpreted	Initiated	Hired
Generated	Identified	Monitored	Formulated	Modeled	Introduced	Innovated	Implemented
Identified	Inspected	Negotiated	Illustrated	Monitored	Lectured	Instituted	Increased
Managed	Installed	Operated	Influenced	Motivated	Mediated	Insured	Inspired
Minimized	Investigated	Organized	Introduced	Negotiated	Modeled	Introduced	Integrated
Negotiated	Maintained	Overhauled	Invented	Outlined	Moderated	Invented	Led
Obtained	Manufactured	Planned	Launched	Persuaded	Modified	Investigated	Managed
Planned	Modified	Prepared	Marketed	Prioritized	Persuaded	Marketed	Operated
Prepared	Operated	Processed	Merchandised	Proposed	Presented	Mastered	Organized
Prevented	Organized	Procured	Obtained	Proposed	Proposed	Obtained	Oversaw
Projected	Overhauled	Purchased	Originated	Publicized	Published	Optimized	Planned
Reconciled	Prescribed	Retained	Performed	Recruited	Recommended	Overcame	Prioritized
Recorded	Programmed	Retrieved	Persuaded	Reported	Reinforced	Pioneered	Produced
Rectified	Regulated	Revamped	Produced	Represented	Relayed	Produced	Promoted
Reduced	Reinforced	Salvaged	Promoted	Resolved	Revised	Ranked	Recommended
Regulated	Repaired	Scheduled	Prompted	Responded	Set	Recognized	Reduced
Researched	Researched	Simplified	Proposed	Retained	Shaped	Reproduced	Reorganized
Researched	Resolved	Specified	Refined	Scheduled	Simplified	Restructured	Represented
Restructured	Restored	Standardized	Researched	Screened	Stimulated	Simplified	Reviewed
Revised	Reviewed	Started	Revamped	Searched	Suggested	Sold	Served
Saved	Solved	Streamlined	Revised	Stimulated	Summarized	Solicited	Solved
Secured	Systematized	Systematized	Segmented	Structured	Taught	Streamlined	Spearheaded
Segmented	Tested	Tabulated	Staged	Terminated	Trained	Succeeded	Sponsored
Selected	Uncovered	Updated	Translated	Trained	Translated	Trained	Strengthened
Tabulated	Upgraded	Utilized	Updated	Tutored	Tutored	Upgraded	Supervised
Verified	Verified	Validated	Visualized	Unified	Wrote	Won	Trained
				Updated			

Chapter 4 Review Questions

1. The primary purpose of your resume, is to get you an interview.

   a) True

   b) False

2. Your resume should be:

   a) A chronological description of all of your activities.

   b) A biographical representation of the major events in your life.

   c) Results oriented and focused to show a fit to the position for which you are applying.

   d) Colorful and include pictures when possible.

   e) All of the above.

3. What is Applicant Tracking System or ATS?

   _____

   _____

   _____

   _____

   _____

   _____

4. How can you insure that your resume will successfully make it through an Applicant Tracking System (ATS)?

   _____

   _____

   _____

   _____

   _____

5. In the space provided insert **your personal** Career Profile as would be appropriate from the discussion in the chapter on Resumes:

_____

_____

_____

_____

_____

_____

6. It is critical that you understand the need for performance/result-oriented bullets after each of the jobs or roles that you list on in your resume. These bullets need to clearly show the impact you made in the role and also address at least in general terms how your action demonstrates a skill that is transferable to the next role you are seeking. Show that you clearly understand how to create a performance/results-oriented bullet that speaks to your personal impact in the last role that you had. This can be from a part-time or full-time role. If you have not had a role where you worked or performed work for someone else consider the last project you worked on. List two bullets from a job, part-time role or project as if you were writing them for your resume:

    a) Your Job, your job's location   Date range of your job

    * _____

    * _____

    * _____

    * _____

7. You are sending your resume to a prospective employer for an internship. This chapter gave many areas to watch, but what are the two major issues that you should be aware of (and address) before you hit the "send" command?

    a) _____

    b) _____

CHAPTER FIVE

ONLINE PROFILE AND YOUR BRAND

W hat is your personal brand and how do others see you? How will someone select you out of all the other candidates for a particular career opportunity? Are you just one in the masses or are you clearly and uniquely qualified for the role you seek?

© blvdone/Shutterstock.com.

How do you distinguish yourself from others? You should know that you have a personal brand, whether you intentionally created it and consistently maintain it or it was created by others based on their interaction with you. Your personal brand may have also developed through the perception of people who have dealt with you or are familiar with your reputation. Everyone has a personal brand, whether you are a top student and the most extroverted person on the planet or you happen to be incredibly introverted and shy.

What can be a game changer for your career is when you actively build and shape your personal brand to show a strong fit for the career role you are seeking. Managing your personal brand and online profile are two very important parts of your career management.

Something that will enhance your personal and professional career management is when you realize that you are truly unique. It is an important part of how you build and shape your personal brand. You may not be aware of it, but it is also a critical ingredient to your personal brand. In this era of everyone receives a trophy for participating, it is easy to consider everyone as "equally qualified." Yet if you do this, you do yourself an injustice. You have a unique set of experiences, interests, and abilities. This personal uniqueness helps form the foundation of your brand and then you build upon that with the direction of your personal and professional career interests. These attributes, along with a keen awareness of what is required to stand out and excel in your career field, can help shape your online profile and your professional brand. Your personal attributes are uniquely you. Do you have a significant work ethic, a desire to make a difference, a willingness to give your best until the task is complete?

When I talk about uniqueness, I am speaking about those environmental experiences that gave you something a little different than your peers. This experience can give you an edge or be a resource you can draw from when others are discouraged. Is it commitment, service, compassion, sensitivity, vision, drive, ability to speak out when others will not, analysis, communication, or one of a hundred other attribute areas? Nobody has the exact same experiences, and we are shaped by those (good and bad). If you have a difficult time evaluating what your attributes are and you feel challenged to define what makes you unique, ask the people who know you the best. Ask them to describe two or three things that sets you apart from others in your family, friends, and others you come in contact with on a regular basis. This is part of your brand.

For me these would have been work ethic and determination. If you asked my family or friends, this would have been a consistent theme. These also followed me into college and into professional life. Taking the primary differentiating attributes and applying them to critical functional job requirements for the position you seek will help you build a brand that will be genuine for you and will give you traction for your career aspirations.

I worked to understand my own personal career assessment when I was in college. I added to this assessment, comments and insight from individuals who worked in the business areas I was interested in. These individuals had advice regarding important job requirements and qualifications. From this analysis, I felt confident the role I would be seeking when I graduated would require the following: supervisory and management skills, attention to detail and commitment to complete each task on time, and without excuse.

Ken Describes his Personal Brand

My ability to describe examples of work ethic and my determination (areas that seemed to set me apart from my peers) supported several of those key requirements. Knowing that I needed supervisory experience, I worked in retail and manufacturing businesses in the summers to establish credibility in these areas. I also gained credibility with attention to detail by targeting roles where I would be closing the business at the end of the day and by preparing cash and credit activity, bank statements, and monthly projections. These activities were gained from a small entrepreneurial business, but it gave me a much better understanding of the job requirements I would need to perform when I graduated.

All of this was done during the summers or holiday breaks, and oftentimes, it was not a full-time job, but something I was doing part-time to build my career credibility and personal brand. I was able to build my personal brand via my resume by including a summary statement regarding my personal unique attributes (work ethic and determination) as well as credible examples of functional experiences that demonstrated the required critical capabilities and qualifications for the role I was seeking. Lastly, I sought out referrals from the people I had worked for in order to lend additional credibility to my personal brand.

These referrals were not simply names and contact information on a sheet of paper, but active referrals who spoke to their friends and peers regarding career opportunities. Many times this would begin with "I am not sure if you have an opening for a new college graduate, but if you do you really should give this guy a look. He has done a great job for us on a part-time basis while going to school and if we had a position available we would hire him."

In the earlier chapters, the career process and how to target career areas that interest you were discussed. You need to be mindful to build credible support that clearly shows you meet the critical qualifications of the career role you seek. If you are wondering what those "critical qualifications" are, they are the primary statements in a job posting under "requirements" or "qualifications."

Many times students want to do something "fun" for their summer or holiday break. Students need to take advantage of at least a portion of that free time to create several success stories for their resumes. There is nothing wrong with "fun," but you need to balance that with building credibility for your career area of interest.

You need to be aware that your brand is more than who you think you are. It is actually more about who others think you are. Almost everyone believes that they are the best for the role they seek and they rationalize that the reason they were not selected for the opportunity is because the person who was evaluating them just did not realize how good they really are. You need a realistic, unbiased perspective on your brand.

Be the person who everyone wants to employ because they not only see statements that speak to your capability (resume) in a directly applicable manner, but when they speak with you by phone or in a face-to-face interview, they are able to hear stories that substantiate your capabilities. When these employers speak to professors who know you, alumni who have met you, and individuals who cross your path during the recruiting and interview process, they hear nothing but positive feedback. They see this and hear this because you have effectively managed your personal brand.

This is not a suggestion to work on your acting skills and portray something you are not. It is simply a suggestion that you know who you are and what makes you special and you know what is required to succeed in the role you seek (you did your homework and research) and you have prepared yourself accordingly. Think back through your college career and remember a time when you were not prepared for the test or assignment. The minute you realized the mistake, anxiety kicked in as did the fear of potential and highly likely failure. You can portray yourself as prepared, but you know you are not. You can fake it and do a wonderful acting job, but you cannot deliver and perform to you potential. However, you also know during your college career when you were prepared and you confidently took the test and did well on the assignment. Your personal brand must be clearly understood by you as well as the impact your brand can make in your career success.

Here are some additional thoughts about "your brand":

- Defines who you are (whether you like it or not)
- It is your reputation
- It is more about how others see you than how you see yourself
- You can maintain, build, or hurt your brand—success and failure are both up to you
- Someone once said, your true personal brand is who you are when you do not think anyone else is looking—your overall, everyday conduct

- It has a lot to do with your dedication, performance, attitude, and energy
- Your brand is also built by what you say as well as what you do not say
- Ask people you know to be honest and direct with how they perceive your personal and professional brand—you want brutally honest assessment from those you respect

Your brand is also made up of many pieces, some of the main ones are:

- Resume/e-mails/texts—formal presence
- Social media—online presence
- First impressions—physical presence
- Actions or lack of actions—observed presence
- Leadership, teamwork, effort—peer presence
- Performance—endorsement presence

Here are a few examples of how the abovementioned pieces are part of your brand. If you struggle with formal communication and tend to use improper grammar (like, . . . I was like, . . . you know, . . . me and Joe worked for, etc.) and make frequent mistakes and misspellings, you will only hurt your professional image. A misspelled word on a resume, application, or cover letter is deal killer. Formal communications can set you apart from your peers. Do not take shortcuts when you communicate with others. Read the e-mail, text, and tweet several times before you hit the "send" button. Action and the lack of action are part of your brand.

Do you volunteer for stretch tasks and duties to make you better or do you stay silent and try and hide in the pack? Your action or lack thereof speaks to your brand. Are you an active participant in your team project assignments or are you the person who feels no responsibility to communicate with your team members and has to be chased down to complete the assigned task? You are building your brand (good and bad) every day. Be aware of this and take an active role in managing your brand to support your career goals.

© Happy Zoe/Shutterstock.com

One of the most important areas for your brand is your online profile. This is what the outside world, friends, peers, and interested recruiters see when they look you up online. What type of web presence do you have? One area that is critical for you to have is a solid, professional LinkedIn profile. Some may argue that this is true for those interested in a career in the business field, but not so for other career fields. I disagree. Regardless of the career field, your path will intersect with business people and your brand will provide additional credibility if you have a solid and updated LinkedIn profile. Your profile should look professional and represent you with a photo that is appropriate for your career area of interest.

You should have an overview below your photo that addresses your career field and speaks to your qualifications and interests. You should have a reasonable amount of professional contacts to legitimize your profile and brand. In my opinion, for an undergrad, this would be a minimum of 100–200 contacts for a junior, 200–300 contacts for a senior, and 300–400 professional contacts for an early career graduate student and an experienced graduate student should have well over 500 contacts. These are not your basic Facebook contacts, but professional contacts with jobs, careers, and professional interests. LinkedIn allows you to search for alumni from your school, and this is a great resource for contacts, as are your professors and professional contacts who come to campus to speak to students in an information session or class. You can also connect to associations that are affiliated with your career area and to companies that are leaders and innovators in your career field. LinkedIn does a great job of connecting people, so take advantage of it.

Go to LinkedIn's home page and search for the LinkedIn Profile Checklist for students. Pay close attention to the instructions so you can make the most out of your profile and LinkedIn presence. This is a great tool and does an exceptional job of assisting you in the creation and management of your LinkedIn profile.

Your LinkedIn profile is a great resource, and you should use it to your best career advantage. There may be new, innovative, and more productive tools in the future, but do not miss out on this one. The landing screen for this link looks like this, and I highly recommend you use this incredible career tool to maximize your LinkedIn presence:

LinkedIn Profile Checklist

□ **PHOTO:** It doesn't have to be fancy - just use your cellphone camera in front of a plain background. Wear a nice shirt and don't forget to smile!

□ **HEADLINE:** Tell people what you're excited about now and the cool things you want to do in the future.

□ **SUMMARY:** Describe what motivates you, what you're skilled at, and what's next.

□ **EXPERIENCE:** List the jobs you held, even if they were part-time, along with what you accomplished at each. Even include photos and videos from your work.

□ **ORGANIZATIONS:** Have you joined any clubs at school or outside? Be sure to describe what you did with each organization.

David Xiao
Econ Major and Aspiring Financial Analyst
San Francisco Bay Area | Financial Services

Previous   Berkeley Ventures
Education   University of California, Berkeley

[Improve your profile] [Edit Profile ▾]   153
                                                    connections

in www.linkedin.com/in/davidxiao/   📇 Contact Info

Background

Summary

I'm a senior at Berkeley, starting to look for roles in the financial industry. As an economics major, I'm fascinated by the invisible forces that shape our world. Why does one company succeed and another fail? Is it possible to predict which idea will be the next big thing?

As such, I've taken lots of microeconomics coursework and have interned with a local venture capital firm. And now I'd like to put that experience to good use, analyzing tomorrow's up-and-coming companies.

Experience

Venture Capital Internship   Berkeley Ventures
Berkeley Ventures
May 2013 – September 2013 (5 months) | Berkeley, CA

Conducted research on 20 startup companies and presented my findings to the fund's board, leading to a new $1.5 million investment.

A presentation I gave to my classmates, based on what I learned at Berkeley Ventures

Organizations

Berkeley A Capella
Lead Singer
March 2012 – Present

Schedule and perform at events for one of Berkeley's oldest a cappella groups, including last year's Cal-Stanford game.

Continued >>

Want more LinkedIn tips for students? Check out students.linkedin.com   **Linked in.**

LinkedIn presence is a must-have for college students. This is a free service and an incredible way to establish and build your personal and professional brand. If you do a great job on the LinkedIn "Checklist," you will be very glad you did.

First and foremost, even though today's job market is much better than it was a few years ago, there are still far too many unemployed and underemployed individuals to compete with you in your internship/job search, so do not be fooled into believing that employers are just looking for warm-blooded, air breathing, average individuals to hire. They want the best of the best, just as you would if the hiring decision was yours to make.

So, what are some things that you can do from an online profile or personal brand perspective to increase the likelihood you will be the person who is selected to interview for the opportunity?

© Elena Elisseeva/Shutterstock.com

To position yourself for the next level and to be able to distinguish your brand above others, you will need to know:

- What motivates, drives, and draws you to perform
- What makes you special and unique for the role you seek
- What your career track looks like and why that is a fit for you
- What the primary duties are for the job/role you seek and how success in this role is measured
- Why you chose and are excited by this industry
- That you can you articulate why you are the best candidate for the job

- Can you back up your credibility for the role with past performance

Be advised that it is hard work to build a strong professional brand and online profile, and if you are not careful, you can lose much of that hardworking image almost overnight. In today's web-based, real-time social microscope, where everyone has a camera on their cell phone, a few moments of indiscretion can be the reason you miss out on a career opportunity that you would otherwise be a great fit for. As a young person seeking your first professional career opportunity after graduation, you should be aware if you are selected for an interview those who are recruiting you will review your background. If you happen to have inappropriate photos or comments posted online, this could be a reason you do not advance to the next level of the interview process.

For many individuals there is a perception that they have the ability to create or become anything they want, and be anything they want to be, with respect to their on-line profile. The reality is that it is very hard to credibly be something you are not. Even non-IT technical types can gain surprisingly complete and genuine profiles from background information available online about you. You should be aware that anything you say or put in print (application, resume, etc.) will be checked and double-checked as will your online social media presence.

It is safe to say, you should assume information that is in the public domain will be accessed and reviewed by recruiters and hiring managers. Your social media footprint is readily discoverable, and you should be aware that things you post, photos you are in, people you are connected to, and interests you have may influence decisions made about your career future.

So who are you? How do you represent yourself? For most college students and young graduates, there is an expectation that you have a large social media image. You need to understand the impact of your online profile and personal brand. It can help you gain an interview or it can eliminate you from consideration.

You might think this is unfair or unethical activity by the employer who is considering you, but you should know they will do everything they can to insure they hire the best, brightest, and highest potential impact candidate they possibly can. Even if you think it is unfair or unethical, be aware that is how you will be measured so adjust accordingly.

Make sure your social media profile represents a person an employer would want on their staff. Here is a photo that would not be viewed as favorable by an employer looking for a young professional:

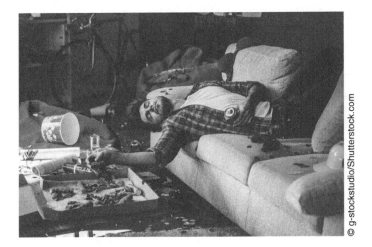

© g-stockstudio/Shutterstock.com

Chapter 5 Review Questions

1. Your personal brand is how YOU see yourself.

    a) True
    b) False

2. The book speaks to an appropriate number of LinkedIn contacts based on your college level. Which letter corresponds to the recommended number of minimum contacts?

    a) Juniors = 100–200 and Seniors 200–300
    b) Freshman = 10–50
    c) Sophomores = 500–600
    d) Early graduate student = 1000
    e) All of the above

3. As a college business student, what is the **most** important social media platform for your career management?

    a) Facebook
    b) LinkedIn
    c) Twitter
    d) CareerShift
    e) Indeed.com

4. Your brand is made up of many pieces including:

    a) Your resume, email, and texts
    b) Your social media
    c) Your first impression and attitude
    d) Your actions or lack of actions
    e) Your leadership, teamwork, and work ethic
    f) Your performance
    g) All of the above

5. Facebook, Pinterest, Snapchat, and Twitter are personal and private social media areas and are off-limits from a

recruiter so you don't need to worry about what you say and post.

a) True

b) False

6. What can **you** do to improve and enhance your personal brand?

Online Presence = _____

_____

_____

_____

Resume and Work History = _____

_____

_____

_____

Communication Skills = _____

_____

_____

_____

Networking and Connections = _____

_____

_____

_____

Attitude and Work Ethic = _____

_____

_____

_____

_____

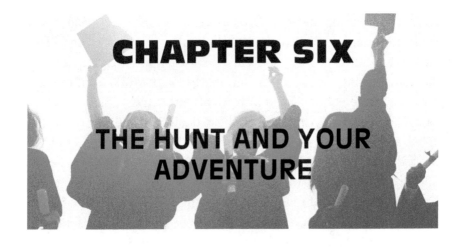

CHAPTER SIX

THE HUNT AND YOUR ADVENTURE

Searching for a college-level internship and/or your first college-level job can be incredibly frustrating. That is why you should "hunt" for an internship or job, not "search" for it. A "Search", is randomly looking for something that is lost but a "Hunt", is a process of preparation, intentional commitment and effort applied to gain what you are seeking. The difference is significant. When you hunt, you diligently and effectively evaluate your objective. You plan, you practice, and you know you have to sacrifice time and effort to be successful. Searching is random and just does not emphasize how important this segment is to your career success. This portion is critical and it takes dedication and commitment to fully realize your potential. How much due diligence or research would you apply to an upcoming vacation, spring break, or for that matter, a long weekend or even a restaurant selection? Most individuals put in a significant amount of research and preparation into these decisions. Yet unfortunately, most students struggle with the same level of engagement on something that is much, much more important, . . . their respective careers. The reason is often because there are so many unknowns and this brings about fear. Fear of the unknown or fear of potential failure leads to procrastination. Take the potential for fear into account and then add to that the fact that students for the most part, feel overwhelmed with the day to day commitments of class, assignments and performance. All of these variables enhance a student's potential to procrastinate when it comes to taking ownership of their respective career development.

We always want you to be aware of what to expect as you "hunt" for your career. We also want you to be aware that making your career a priority requires a significant commitment and this commitment is often without a quick reward. The exciting part is experience breeds confidence and the only way to gain experience is to become engaged in the process.

Have courage and be willing to take those first steps. Have an attitude that recognizes this as a process and with each step you become better and more proficient. Those steps will lead you to success. Look at your career development as a "hunt" that will become more efficient and effective as you dedicate time to it. We can't encourage you enough to take personal ownership of this process, to become informed and committed in the "hunt" will set you apart from your peers.

Begin this process as soon as possible because the sooner you are engaged the sooner you can take advantage of opportunities that are presented to you on an almost daily basis. When you do this you will quickly learn best practices, insights, skills and capabilities that will help you excel in your job or internship "hunt"

Do you have the heart and determination to send out 100 updated resumes and applications to positions for which you strongly believe you are a fit? Hard work and dedication as well as solid internship experience might reward you with a full-time job in as few as 10 applications, but you had better be prepared for 100 if that is what it takes. Remember the chapter on Attitude, This is Your Career, Your Future so recognize what is at stake and treat this hunt as your next adventure.

What should a student expect as they prepare to succeed in their career "hunt"? We would estimate the time our more successful and active students put into their career management including: self-assessment, career discovery and analysis, role research, resume building, internship and job hunting, networking, connecting, and interview preparation would amount to nearly 10 hours compared to each hour actually spent in an interview with the recruiter or company when they begin.

That amount of time may shock you or even create an extra measure of anxiety or frustration. Hundreds of applicants will most likely apply for the roles you seek and often only a handful are selected for an interview and a smaller number are given official internship or job offers. You have to make a commitment to put in the time in order to set yourself apart from the other applicants. Also, once you have a successful "hunt" for the first time and you discover a potential employer that is genuinely interested in you, it will all be worth it.

Students over the years have shown time and time again, once you have your first successful "hunt", you will realize the value of the practice and preparation and you work that much harder to improve your skills. In addition, once you gain experience in this process, your time will be spent actually in the "hunt" along with networking, connecting, and the interview preparation portion. You should also be aware that most face-to-face interviews include multiple interviewers, recruiters, and hiring managers and this can easily stretch an interview to two to three hours. Your preparation time will likely increase, accordingly.

Your job or internship "hunt" follows this same path with respect to preparation. Let's assume you know your skills, strengths, and weaknesses, as well as your unique attributes and the things that set you apart. You have a clear idea about what you want to do and what type of internship or job role you would like to play. You know the type of industry that appeals to you and the type of company and culture you believe you will enjoy. You plan, you scout, and you practice. You do work and preparation so that when you have an opportunity to take advantage of something that is much more than a hobby (your career), you will be successful.

Let us take a look at what your personal career "hunt" might look like. What is the career role that you want to hunt? Is it a marketing, education, sales, finance, coaching, engineering, management, accounting, operations, administrative, scientist, human resources, doctor, lawyer, healthcare specialist, law enforcement, or any number of other roles that you are interested in or excited about? Recall from Chapter 2 on Attitude and Your Dream Job that you just make the best choice you can with the information you have at that time. You may change your mind later as you learn more about what you like and dislike about the role. The important thing is to get started.

Decide what career role you want to hunt. Then decide on the location or area you want to hunt. You should target the area or location that is as best you can tell is the most desired location for you to live when you graduate. You should, however, be open to other locations if they have significantly better opportunities.

Ken Buckley's career perspective - I am a native Texan and as many of you have probably heard, Texans typically like to stay in Texas. I stayed in Texas when I graduated college for several years, but I knew that in the technology industry I had chosen, I needed to go to California as that was where technology and innovation were at their peak at the time of my graduation. I knew it would be different from Texas, but I also knew if I wanted to truly advance my career I should go where there was a chance to tackle bigger opportunities. You should too. So decide where you want to hunt, but be open to going outside your comfort zone if you believe it will significantly boost your career and experience. Then plan your hunt and your adventure and go.

One great way to know the potential opportunities that exist in the area you are interested in, even if you have never been there before, is to talk to people in those areas who are family, family friends, alums, or contacts (Facebook, LinkedIn, etc.). They can provide insight into the opportunities and demographics of the area.

When I decided to go to California from Texas to gain experience in a higher growth company with a role of increased responsibility, I spoke with contacts I had in the industry who lived in California. They helped provide insight into my decision and gave me a perspective I would not have had, since I had never lived outside of Texas.

Part of this chapter is about "Adventure" and one key ingredient of adventure is change. Change is never easy and for most people change is fine as long as someone else has to do it. There is an old expression, "the only person that really wants change is a wet baby." Change is always a challenge, but you should treat your internship and job "hunt" as an adventure and be not only open to change, but expect it and even embrace it, you will be very glad you did and your career will be much better for it. Young professionals can grow by taking stretch assignments and challenging responsibilities, by being willing to relocate, by being willing to travel and work internationally, and by realizing that each adventure involves a large measure of change.

When you have chosen the role you want as well as where you want to live, your next step is to prepare and equip yourself for success. You need to fully prepare for your hunt the same way.

Make sure you are prepared and confident. Is this the first time you are wearing this specific suit or dress (beware the wardrobe problems)? Are you sure you have left plenty of time to arrive at your interview (at least fifteen minutes early, by the way)? Do you have gas in the car? Will you remember to turn your cell phone off? Did you make extra copies of your resume? Have you practiced for the interview in front of the mirror and had a friend, family member, career staff member or faculty ask you difficult interview questions? Be prepared and do not take shortcuts.

Have your resume, your elevator speech/personal introduction, your interview preparation, and engaging, well-thought out questions for the recruiter planned, prepared and rehearsed well in advance. In addition, as part of your interview preparation can you effectively answer these challenging questions:

- Why is this internship or job role perfect for you?
- Why do you consider yourself the best candidate for the role?
- Why do you think this company is the right one for you?
- Why do you think the company should hire you over the other applicants?
- Why do you believe this industry is exciting?

If you can successfully answer these questions you are well on your way to being prepared. You may have seen a few of these questions early in the book, but they are here again to show the significance. Remember, in each interview whether formal or informal you do not get a "do-over" or a chance to make another "first impression."

The job or internship "hunt" is a complex and challenging process, but let's try and simplify it.

We will break it down into three strategies areas:

1. Internet-based hunting: Let us assume you are a business major and have decided on a business role, and so begin a key word "hunt" on www.careershift.com, www.indeed.com, your university online recruiting portal, or a general internet search for the internship or job that you want to pursue. To make this as efficient as possible, use keywords to focus your hunt such as "degree" (so that you are looking at college opportunities), and you then input one or two functional skills such as marketing, project management, analysis, operations, and so on, as well as the location that you have selected. You can normally do this by major metropolitan area or zip code and often you can provide a mileage range around the area. When you hit the "Return" button on your internet-based hunting adventure, you will likely get a large amount of internship or job options. This could be literally hundreds of opportunities. You can either refine your search with additional keywords or go through the opportunities until you find several that seem like a great fit for you.

This is casting a broad net and even though it is the easiest strategy to implement, it is also where most students become very frustrated with the career management process. It is very important part of your overall scouting strategy and trust me it will help you refine and reshape your role. You will see many different descriptions of the role you are seeking and this will help inform you of what is required to be considered fully qualified for the role and it will also inform you of the basic duties and tasks that must be performed in the role.

2. Targeted hunting: Keeping in mind the previous assumptions you used as you searched for your role from internet-based hunting, the difference in Internet-based hunting and targeted hunting is that your target becomes more company or employer-focused, as well as role-focused. You target the career Web sites of companies that you are interested in for the roles you want to pursue. You are not just looking at roles that are a possible fit in a large geographic area; instead, you are looking for a specific internship or job title within a specific company or group of companies. You target the role after you have learned more about the qualifications and requirements and through this refinement you become more precise in your selection. You can also research the companies based on their size in revenue, employee headcount, corporate location, public ownership (they are listed on the stock market like IBM, AT&T, etc.) or private ownership (Mars, Dell, HE Butt Grocery, Ernst & Young, etc.), employee satisfaction ranking, industry they serve, products or services they provide, and any other area that helps you find a connection that makes the company desirable. Targeted hunting is more efficient, but if you do not have some solid experience with internet-based hunting you will limit your success as well as the potential of the targeted hunt.

Taking advantage of your university career fairs would be considered targeted hunting. You have a location (your campus) and you have an abundance of employers available that are university-friendly and committed to recruiting at your campus. They have spent time and money to be on your campus and you DEFINITELY need to take advantage of that opportunity. You should do the same work with respect to focusing on the employers and the roles that are a fit for you.

When other employers are on campus and they either do not have a posted opportunity on your university recruiting site or they happen to be a firm that you have not previously considered . . . do yourself and your career a favor and research them. Many, many times, employers come to campus for specific roles, and have a significant amount of college-level opportunities posted on their Web site, but not on the university recruiting site. You will not know these opportunities exist unless you review the employer's career page on their Web site. The recruiters that are on campus may not be there to recruit for those positions, but they can often provide direction on how to reach the individuals that are responsible. They can also share insight into the recruiting process and provide information that will help your resume or application get noticed. Campus recruiting is one of the areas that I think will change significantly over the years, but take advantage of it and consider it targeted hunting.

3. **Guided hunts:** Keeping with what you did in the Internet-based hunting and targeted hunting, you bring to bear another level of expertise to your career management process. You now have an improved knowledge of the requirements and qualifications of the role you seek along with an increased understanding of the location and companies that seem like a great fit for you. With this added knowledge, you adjust your resume to show as a strong fit for the desired roles as much as possible and then you bring in a person with experience with the role, the company or the industry as your subject matter expert. Your guide is one of the most important assets you can have. He or she has the ability of greatly multiplying your potential hunting success.

Your guide is someone who knows you or knows of you through family, friends, and acquaintances. These individuals need to know your interests and they also need to have your resume. Giving them an electronic copy is preferred so that they can easily share it with others. To secure a guide's service from someone you know or that knows of you, you normally only have to say something like: "I am looking for an internship (or job) and I would appreciate your insight and wisdom to look over my resume and let me know what you think." You are not asking them for an internship or a job, just their insight. Most of the guides will easily accept and many will not only look over your resume, but will network on your behalf to connect you to opportunities that they believe may be a fit. Or they will connect you to someone they believe will have more information or can provide better assistance.

Guided hunts are your best bet for success. However, if you do not put in the work on the Internet-based hunt and the targeted hunt your success for a guided hunt will be significantly limited. Do the work and you will enjoy the rewards.

You should also know that there are recruiting seasons. When you hunt for your internship you should know that employers who have top-flight internships are recruiting for these upcoming summer (for example) positions are receiving applications for those opportunities in the fall of the previous year. If you are interested in a government or select nonprofit role, this might be a year in advance. You should start your hunt at least nine months before you hope to start your role, twelve months if possible.

So if you are seeking a summer internship you should be ready to engage with your "hunt" strategy beginning in the fall prior to the summer at the latest. If you are graduating in the May or December time frame give yourself a full twelve months to position yourself for success. If you are reading this and you graduate in a month, you obviously do not have twelve months to work with. Do not hit the panic switch; just know that you will have to work even harder to make up for lost time. No matter the situation, you can only give your best and take care of the things that are under your control. Begin the "hunt" as soon as possible and then work diligently to move as quickly as possible to the "guided hunt."

Keep a spreadsheet on your "hunts." Here is a screenshot of a basic tracking sheet we use with our students. We have provided headings in the spreadsheet, but feel free to modify the headings and other areas to best support your career development. If you create and maintain a spreadsheet you will be far more effective in your career "hunt". Your chances of accomplishing your goals (career or personal) go up significantly if you write them down and actively manage them. Take ownership of your "hunt" and realize that you and you alone are accountable for your career success.

Internship/Job Hunt Strategy and Tracking

My Targets and Top Priority

POSITION	COMPANY	Link or Where Applied	Date Applied	Contact	Resume Sent	Cover Ltr Sent	Fit Y!N	Response Y!N	Interview Y!N	Offer Y!N	Comments

As we close the chapter on The Job Hunt and Your Adventure, international students should take note of the following tip. If you are an international student that is seeking employment in the United States you will have additional challenges to your job/internship hunt. There is a great book specifically directed to the career needs of international students. The book is titled Power Ties, The International Student's Guide to Finding a Job in the United States by Dan Beaudry. If you are an international student you should read Dan Beaudry's book. It is an excellent source of career information. Many international students we have worked with struggle with networking, communication and connecting. This book does a nice job of addressing these challenges and others.

This last page of this chapter happens to have a target with an arrow in the middle of it. The words Your Career are at the top and then there are three other blocks of words around the target. All of these items come together to create an example of what your personal career adventure can look like. Each of the segments is important and you need to research them accordingly. Some are internal and require self-reflection, honest assessment by yourself and those you respect, as well as a comparison or gap analysis of what you have compared to what is required to be the leading candidate for the role you are "hunting." Some of the words are external in nature and require you to actively research your respective career marketplace.

When you have confidently and diligently done these things, you need to practice and prepare so that each time you get a shot at an opportunity you can be successful. Remember, it is very unlikely that you will know from the first minute you decide to engage with your career development with 100% certainty what you truly want to do when you graduate. You need to look at each opportunity from a fresh perspective, research, prepare and then be willing to apply yourself to succeed. The next employer information session, career fair or job posting may be door opener to your career dreams.

Get ready for the hunt of your lifetime.

Your "Career"

Your Skills, Experience, Capabilities

Your Passion, Interests, Attitude

Job Market, Opportunities, Hiring Trends, Change

Chapter 6 Review Questions

1. The book says that a job or internship "hunt" is much more intentional than a job or internship "search".

   a) True
   b) False

2. This chapters states that normally, the only person who wants change is a

   a) Realist
   b) Pessimist
   c) Wet baby
   d) Your parents

3. The book spoke about three forms of job/internship searches and described them as different hunts. Which method normally yields the greatest success and why?

   a) Targeted hunts
   b) Guided hunts
   c) Internet-based hunts

   Why is this method normally the best? _____

   _____

   _____

   _____

4. What can you do now to become more comfortable with change? Describe what **you** can personally do to improve your attitude to see change as not only a major catalyst for your career success, but a gateway to an exciting adventure?

   _____

   _____

   _____

   _____

5. What is the difference between Target hunting and Internet-based hunting?

_____

_____

6. Your job/internship "hunt" will not be successful unless you commit some time and effort into the discovery of what you want to do and some energy into the planning, preparation, and execution of the "hunt". Your career adventure is one of the primary reasons you are attending college. Take ownership of your career by answering the following questions:

What are you going to "hunt" for as your career role?

a) List the job/internship title that you will seek now or when you graduate: _____

_____

_____

Where do you want to live?

b) _____

What companies are you interested in and would like to work for?

c) _____

What are the primary skills and qualifications required for the job/internship title you listed in a)?

d) _____

_____

_____

Who do you know that can be a resource for learning more about your job/internship title, location you want to live, companies you are interested, and providing overall career support?

e) _____

_____

_____

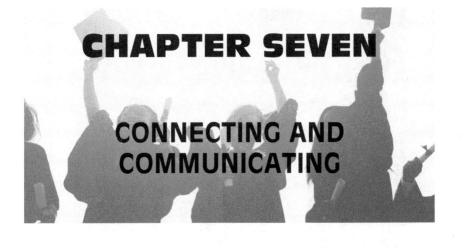

CHAPTER SEVEN

CONNECTING AND COMMUNICATING

© mast3r/Shutterstock.com

Y ou may be one of those students who easily meets people and has always been the most popular student in the class or on campus, but for most students connecting and communicating is a challenge. Connecting and communicating is a vital and critical part of your career management. In truth, these two areas cause quite a bit of anxiety with most students, but hopefully, after this chapter you will find it much easier to become a polished professional at both.

© Rawpixel.com/Shutterstock.com

Let's start with connecting: When you are in college you will have an opportunity to meet and connect with so many individuals. A large number of these individuals can have a measurable impact on your career. However, most students feel uncomfortable asking people to do things for them when they really don't know them. This is one of the most common concerns and frustrations that students experience when they think of connecting or networking. Hopefully by helping you see things from the other person's perspective it will explain why there is a better strategy to use when you are trying to "connect" with people you do not know, in order to support your career. To understand the other person's perspective, if you recommended a student or person to a business associate and that individual turns out to be a "dud" or nonperformer, then your overall business credibility is as suspect as the judgment you used when you made the recommendation.

So if you think connecting is asking someone to recommend you or give you a job when they know nothing about you, then it makes sense that you would be anxious and frustrated. The concern and frustration is justified if you expect people who have no connection with you to spend their valuable time recommending someone that they know nothing about to individuals whose relationships are strategic to their livelihood.

However, here is the game changer, you are not asking for a recommendation or a position with their company or a position with people with which they are connected. Your initial connection is much more subtle than this.

This should help put the difference into perspective. You are in class and your professor speaks about her experience on a recent project that just happens to be in an area in which you are interested. After class you ask the professor a question about the experience and after she addresses your question you add a follow-up question, "If you were interested in working in that industry, what would you recommend that you do if you were a sophomore (or junior, etc.) in college to better prepare?"

You will probably be surprised by the answers you receive. Not because you are helped by a faculty member who seems to be very busy, but surprised by how easy it was to enter into the discussion and discover something valuable about your career path. You will also be surprised by the fact that you might even be introduced by at least an email from your professor to someone in that industry, if your interest was sincere.

Here is another example to further clarify how to connect. At the invitation of your professor, a speaker comes into your classroom to talk about his experiences in coordination with a class activity you are having. You can be sure there will be a time for questions. If you have prepared appropriately and researched the individual and his company (as you should with any speaker coming to your class) you will take advantage of the opportunity and ask an interesting and thought provoking question. If you cannot think of one, a safe bet is always, "How did you get your start in this industry and what words of wisdom or insight would you have for someone looking to follow a similar career path?" You can modify this as you need to, but the point is you should be able to ask a question like this without being overcome by anxiety and stress.

You have to practice speaking in a group setting to gain confidence in that type of environment, so do not be confused by the stress or anxiety from speaking out in a group versus connecting. They are very different. You are not expected to suddenly feel free of any stress when there is still a public speaking issue, but you should expect to feel confident instead of stressed with respect to the question or questions you ask. These questions may have an exciting impact on your career.

Be aware of the potential you have by asking career-related questions to individuals who have more experience than you. If you look around outside of your college classroom it is almost everyone you might meet. Slight exaggeration, but the point is most people, especially alumni, individuals connected to your university, faculty/staff, as well as your family and friends are very willing to share insight when asked in a manner that does not require them to automatically add something to their already loaded "to-do" list.

You should also reach out to those types of contacts via platforms like LinkedIn (remember from earlier chapters how important this platform can be to your career) with similar types of questions. You should also read and follow the connecting strategy highlighted in the book *The Power of Who*. If you want the highest hit rate on your connecting efforts, then go to the individuals that know and care about you the most. *The Power of Who* does an excellent job of breaking these segments down for you. You become clear on what you want to do, to the best of your ability and then you make sure those that know and care about you the most are aware of your interests. You are not necessarily assigning anyone action items, you are simply asking for their input, insight, or advice with respect to an area they have more knowledge and experience than you have.

In the book, The Power of Who, the author surprises his audience by stating that they already know everyone that they need to know. He goes on to explain that close friends, parents, relatives and even acquaintances are connected with people in numerous roles within a wide variety of industries that they are often willing to introduce you to. The more your personal connections know about your career intentions, the better chance you have at increasing your network to include those who can directly impact your employability.

For example, you have conversations almost daily with your friends and parents. Many times, those conversations migrate to talking about school and classroom activities. You should also be talking about your career aspirations - what you want to do, how your schooling is helping you get to that point, and where you could potentially end up. Your contacts might know people who work in those areas or in companies that have jobs in those areas. And sometimes, all it takes is for you to ask your connection, "Do you know anyone who does this type of work?" While your connection might not know immediately, you will have successfully conveyed the message that you are interested in meeting people who work in that professional field. Your conversation won't end at that point, instead, you can go back to it the next time you talk.

Perhaps you look through your connections contacts on LinkedIn and notice someone at a company that you have an interest in. What would stop you from calling your connection (friend or relative) and asking him to introduce you to his contact?

When I knew or felt confident that I wanted to build a career in the technology industry I spoke to several individuals about my interest. The individuals I spoke to were not especially close to me from a friend or association perspective. These were people who worked in business roles of authority above me. I did not work for them, but did say hello on a daily basis as we passed in the hallway or in a company setting. I "connected" with those individuals at different times, through general questions about their experiences and after listening to a few of their industry war stories and personal accomplishments I felt I had a chance to ask them a "non-threatening" career-related question. I asked them, if they were in my situation with a general business degree (marketing) and wanted to build a career in marketing within the technology field, what they would recommend. They, independently, directed me to people who had done just that, as well as, people who hired individuals for those types of roles to better clarify the expectations and qualifications of the role.

It was an invaluable experience and I know I would not have gained the career traction I gained without their insight. Connecting with others by asking general interest-related questions so that you can easily ask nonthreatening career-related questions is a connecting strategy that will benefit you throughout your career.

The benefits of connecting and building informal relationships and then asking nonthreatening career-related questions is something that every student can use regardless of their major or career direction. There are times though, that a much more direct approach to connecting is needed. If you have never had to actually change a flat tire before, on your own, and you happen to find yourself with a flat tire in an area without phone coverage, you will appreciate this.

Here is a picture of a person who has never experienced changing their own flat. They looked over the owner's manual, but have no idea how to actually begin the process and change the tire.

Viacheslav Nikolaenko/Shutterstock.com

You can easily read the manual that comes with your vehicle in time of need, but reading the manual and intellectually comprehending what is written is a far cry from actually changing the flat. If you have a flat and you are on your own and or do not have cell coverage to call for help, you must take matters into your own hands or be "stranded." If on the other hand you have actually changed a flat tire you will be (literally) miles ahead of someone who has not. Putting what you have read into practice (and practicing it) greatly increases your ability to perform the task compared to only the mental acknowledgement of reading it.

The following picture shows a person who not only read about changing a flat they actually had to practice changing one as part of their driver training. When unfortunately, they had a flat on the open road they were experienced and able to change their own flat.

© Corepics VOF/Shutterstock.com

The flat tire story may seem random for this book, but in truth, the reason you need to know how to change your own tire is a tight parallel to a connecting assignment is used in our MBA career courses.

Each year, Baylor MBA students take a week-long career trek to New York City. One of the tasks they must complete it to formally reach out and connect with someone under the following circumstances:

(A) The person must be actively engaged in the student's career field, but be unknown to the student prior to the assignment

(B) The person must hold a position of authority and have legitimate experience within the functional career role they desire

(C) The person must work and have an office in downtown, NYC

(D) They must meet the person during a designated time period that is set before the trip. They cannot meet outside of that time period.

(E) After the meeting they must bring back to a roundtable of faculty and staff a business card from their contact and discuss the meeting in detail.

This creates a large amount of stress because everything has to be completed as stated above; there are no adjustments or allowances for mistakes. The contact has to be approved prior to the trip. The weeklong career trek is also part of a graded career activity. If you complete the assignment you receive a passing grade on that portion of the career trek and if you do not complete the assignment you receive a failing grade for that portion of the trip.

This may seem harsh and it certainly creates pressure on the students to perform a career networking feat, upon completion, most students believe the stress and pressure are worth it - just like it is important for you to actually experience how to change your own flat tire. Here is why. There may come a time when you are looking for work, out of work, in a work transition period and experiencing many economic variables out of your control. The job market may be awful, the weather is terrible, there could be another 9/11. You just do not know what tomorrow holds and you might need to actively and even aggressively position yourself for gainful employment. Your family, your finances or something else that is important might be on the line. The point is sometimes things happen out of your control (like a flat tire) and you must be able to deal with the adversity and rise above it.

To give the MBA students who face this NYC career trek connecting assignment a reasonable chance of success we give them a chance to "read the owner's manual and practice changing the tire" before they have to do it in a stress situation. The student has already gone through a significant amount of class and practice with respect to connecting and they have been trained and have demonstrated their proficiency using career tools that are specifically aligned for connecting. They have done everything they need to do in the classroom (again, very similar to reading the manual on changing a flat tire), but career management is much more about what happens outside the classroom in a real and practical setting.

Although the students struggle with this assignment and the uncertainty of it, they know that it is well worth the challenge they face and stress they experience. This is based on the heightened levels of confidence when they come back and report to the faculty and staff how their connection meeting went. They are not only much more confident but they have learned and applied a very critical career survival tool. They have proven they can connect in a meaningful way with someone (whom they have never met before) that can make a difference in their career. They can accomplish this in an area or location that they likely have never been before and, more importantly, they accomplished this task within a very tight inflexible, timetable.

In this day and age of changes and flexibility, you can image the pressure from worrying about last minute changes so . . . the students are highly encouraged to have multiple appointments just in case their first choice has to fly to Asia to handle a client, or is called into a board meeting or has a personal issue come up.

All of these things happen frequently in business and are quite frequent in NYC. So it is a challenging connecting assignment for sure and our students tackle it and give it their best.

That assignment establishes a connection experience with someone with which you have no prior relationship. It is a challenge that makes you much more capable with respect to your career survival skills. This type of connection is the exception not the rule. The majority of your connecting time should be with individuals who you have at least some relationship with (family, friends, friends of friends, classmates, faculty, staff, alums, fraternity, sorority, church, community involvement, hobby, etc.) that was discussed earlier in the chapter.

One other area of career connecting that is often overlooked is the need to take advantage of industry associations. The membership in associations will allow you to be much more informed about your career field, the industry it serves, and even the functional roles that exist within it. Normally, the associations are free to join and provide a wealth of knowledge with respect to the happenings in the industry. It is another great way to give you an edge compared to your peers.

Here are a few associations for most general business, engineering, and technical interests (there are more being added all the time, believe it or not):

Finance & Accounting	IT/MIS
American Accounting Association (AAA)	Association for Computer Machinery (ACM)
American Bankers Association (ABA)	Association for Information Technology Professionals
American Finance Association (AFA)	

American Institute of Certified Public Accountants (AICPA)	IEEE Computer Society
Association for Financial Professionals (AFP)	Information Systems Audit & Control Association
CFA Institute	Institute for Ops Research & the Management Sciences
Financial Executive International	
Financial Management Association (FMA)	Institute of Electrical & Electronics Engineers
Institute of Management Accountants (IMA)	Society for Information Management
National Association for Business Economics (NABE)	
National Bankers Association (NBA)	
Human Resources	**Marketing**
American Society for Training and Development (ASTD)	American Advertising Federation
American Staffing Association (ASA)	American Marketing Association
HR Southwest (HRSW)	Commercial Development & Marketing Association
Human Resource Planning Society (HRPS)	
International Association for Human Resource Information Management (IHRIM)	Marketing Research Association
	National Association of Sales Professionals
International Public Management Association for HR (IPMAHR)	Qualitative Research Consultants Association

National Association of Professional Employer Organizations (NAPEO) Society for Human Resource Management (SHRM)	**National Nonprofit Associations** National Council of Nonprofit Associations (NCNA) **Nonprofit Management Associations** American Society of Association Executives Alliance of Nonprofit Management
Engineering	**Supply Chain/Operations**
National Society of Professional Engineers (NSPE) American Society of Civil Engineers (ASCE) American Society of Mechanical Engineers (ASME) Institute of Electrical and Electronics Engineers (IEEE)	American Production and Inventory Control Society (APICS) American Society of Transportation and Logistics (ASTL) Association of Professional Material Handling Consultants (APMHC) Council of Supply Chain Management Professionals (CSCMP)
Institute of Industrial Engineers (IIE) Society of Manufacturing Engineers (SME) National Society of Black Engineers (NSBE) Society of Women Engineers (SWE)	Institute for Supply Management (ISM) Supply Chain Council (SCC) The International Society of Logistics (SOLE)

Society of Hispanic Professional Engineers (SHPE)	Strategic Management Society (SMS)
	Association of Change Management (ACMP)
	American Management Association (AMA)

You can search these associations on the web and register/connect. This will give you additional insight into the roles and expectations as well as the leading issues facing this career field. The more you know the better prepared you will be when you talk with someone who is involved in your field of interest.

Let us move from connecting to communicating.

You should be aware of the importance of clear, concise, professional communication and should be continually looking for ways to set yourself apart from your peer competition when it comes to your career management. Today's students are very bright, but oftentimes their communication to individuals who potentially have influence over their careers is filled with abbreviations (LOL, OMG, etc.), slang, improper grammar, misspelled words, and tendency to think the speed of our communication is far more important than the quality of the content.

Here are some basic tips you should follow at all times when communicating by e-mail with respect to your career.

> ➤ Keep your e-mails brief (less than 1/2 page), professional in tone and review the spelling, content, sentence structure, and clarity of your e-mail at least three times before you hit the "send" button.

Example:

Dear Ms. Jane Smith,

Thank you for speaking to our marketing class today. Your description of the challenges of successfully marketing the product ABC in a down market was impressive.

I would love to better position myself for a career in consumer product marketing when I graduate. I know you must be very busy, but I wonder if you would share with me, at your convenience, some things that would set a new college graduate apart from the other candidates.

Once again, I can't thank you enough for taking time to speak in our class and I really appreciate your insight and direction. I am available at your convenience by phone or e-mail.

Respectfully,
Jake Adams
Marketing Major
Class of 20XX
Your University
Jake.Adams@university.edu
254.333.1313

➤ Address the person you are sending the e-mail to in a professional manner. Dear Mr., Mrs., Ms. First name and last name, etc. and NOT Joe, Jane, or other first name until the person gives you permission to address them in this way. You should always treat the person you are speaking to or addressing in an e-mail or formal correspondence with respect.

➤ Do not waste someone's time with things that do not matter. Review the e-mail and remove any fluff or words that can confuse the meaning of the e-mail.

➤ Never assume that the person you are addressing owes you their attention, their time, or their action on your behalf. Be respectful of their time and their position and you will receive more responses.

➤ Never "reply all" to an e-mail list of many names as this is a waste of individual's time and e-mail space. If you have something to say to someone or to a specific group of individuals then by all means do it, but do not hit "reply all" to 50 people you do not know with an off-the-wall comment. One of those 50 may be close friends to the person you just slammed in your comment. E-mails live long lives and sometimes things said in jest can appear disrespectful, hurtful, or malicious when reviewed later by "others."

➤ Beware the dreaded "auto complete" this is a feature where your e-mail address fills in after you type a few characters. You think you are responding to your friend Bob about the "dumb" interview call you just had with Robert at XYZ company and when you hit the address field you start to type Bob. You are in a hurry and do not notice that the auto complete just filled in the name of Robert instead of Bob and you hit send . . . too late to realize you just told the person that interviewed you that you were "not impressed by their interview questions." This happens more than you can imagine so do not send anything until you are sure where it is going and have verified it at least two times.

➤ Always use spell check and grammar check, but be aware that you can spell a word correctly and it can be used improperly in your sentence. You can enable spell and grammar check in your email settings so that this is checked before you actually send the email.

When communicating by phone there are many things to consider as well. For one thing, make sure your voice mail has a professional response to incoming calls. When recruiters or hiring managers try and reach you by phone you want to make sure they leave with a positive opinion or your personal brand. Keep your voice mail response brief and professional and check your messages often. Be careful with texts as you may mistake an incoming message from a recruiter for a friend and fire off a nonprofessional response. As stated previously with e-mails, if you are communicating by text avoid slang and quick answers that miss the point. Read and re-read your messages before you hit the send button to make sure they represent you in best possible manner.

It is likely that your first interview will be a phone interview. With this communication opportunity, there are several ways to enhance your assessment from the recruiter. When you have a scheduled phone interview:

➤ Dress as if you are going to a formal interview—you will feel more professional and conduct yourself accordingly

➤ Stand when you speak on the phone as it will give you more confidence in your tone

➤ Prior to the call make sure you have a copy of your resume, the job or internship posting, recent company news, a copy of the questions you want to ask the interviewer, and your application laid out conveniently for your review during the call

➤ If you have a clock or cell phone nearby, try to keep your answers under a minute to a minute and a half in length

➤ Make sure your cell phone is fully charged

➤ Make sure the room where you take the call is private and there is no television, radio, dog or loud noises that will distract you

➤ Be ready for the call at least 15 minutes prior to the call and if you are calling into the recruiter call in 5 minutes early

➤ Double check the phone number and dialing instructions to make sure you have an active phone number and complete access code

➤ If possible, block off an hour prior to the call so you can focus on the upcoming call and review your notes and interview strategy

➤ Smile while you talk, it will help you bring energy to the call

With respect to more formal and written communications, here are some examples of formal types of correspondence that will assist you with your career management connecting and communicating efforts:

Should you write a cover letter? Always write a cover letter if you have that option. As you will see in the two samples and in the overview, a solid cover letter will give you a much better chance at being noticed. You may not be required or even given an option to include a cover letter with your application for a position, but if you can include one by all means do it. Anytime you have an option to build your brand with a recruiter or hiring manager take advantage of it.

There are many styles and formats for cover letters, but probably the most compelling is a comparison cover letter. In this format you provide a sentence or two of an introduction as well as a closing, but the special part of this format is your comparison of your qualifications to the posted job or internship requirements. This tells a recruiter up front that you are qualified and that you meet or exceed their posted/published requirements. It shows you know what they are looking for and that you are a strong fit. Your resume should also back this up. Here is the example of the "comparison" cover letter:

Cover Letter for an Advertised Opening with a large airline company

March 30, 20XX

Dear Mr. Bob Johnston,

I was very excited to hear about your leaders in training rotational program position from Sam Smith, Director of Human Resources, when he spoke at our undergraduate business case competition, on campus. I feel that I thrive in environments that are largely cross functional, and have had a long-standing passion for your company and the aviation industry it serves.

I feel my background is well suited for the position as detailed below:

Your Requirements:	My Skills/Accomplishments:
• Ability to lead and manage peer groups	• Night manager of restaurant—managed staff of 6, promoted and recognized for business growth
• Track record of success	• College athlete and 2 year starter on Div. 1 football team—2nd team Academic All-Conference
• Demonstrated interest in airlines	• Avid flyer and certified pilot
• Demonstrated leadership on campus/community	• Social chairperson of XXXXXXXX fraternity and logged over 200 hours of community service
• Consumer products or services background	• 2 years working as waiter while full-time in school
• Strong communicator, analytical and interpersonal skills	• 2014 2nd place award at the undergrad case competition against 36 other teams
• Interested in careers with global presence	• Traveled to 4 different countries to support missions work and underprivileged children
• Geographic mobility preferred	• Thrive in 50–75% travel environments
• GPA 3.0 or better	• Currently retain a GPA of 3.45

I am looking forward to an opportunity to interview for this position and I am available at your convenience by phone or in person. If there are additional questions as to my qualifications or background, please do not hesitate to let me know.

Thank you in advance for your time and consideration.

John Smith
Class of 20XX
Management Major
Your University
John.a.smith@university.edu
254.333.6565

Another style of cover letter is a "bullet" style and it makes the career matching points. This is a good style and is often used when you do not have quite the strong fit for all of the qualifications as previously listed in the "comparison" style. You may notice that even though you are capturing your points in "bullets" the document tends to have more text than the "comparison" format.

Cover Letter for an Advertised Opening

April 22, 20XX

Dear Mr. Tom Jango,

In my search for opportunities within ABC, Inc., I discovered the Operations Manager, Reseller Support role to be especially interesting. I am passionate about operations management and have competencies that match up well with the demands of this role.

Some of my relevant experience for the position include:

- Gained extensive cross-cultural project management skills as I led an international consulting team composed of six summer interns in 2013 to develop innovative cost reduction and efficiency improvement solutions for one of ABC, Inc.'s major suppliers, Acme Industries. These solutions equated to roughly $200,000 in savings over the first two years and a reduction of response time to customer service issues by 22% for first time callers.

- Developed strong analytical skills by spending two summers (summers 2011 and 2012) as an operations analyst in training and was a member of numerous data-driven projects across the organization (Supply Chain, Marketing, IT, and Finance).

- Combined experiences as a part-time retail store representative for one of the largest clothing firms in the region with my time in college, serving as a trainer on our university athletic program. Both of these environments are very fast paced. This taught me how to quickly analyze situations, adapt to change, and deliver actionable direction to critical stakeholders.

I believe that my background in operations management, coupled with my analytical approach and experience working in multicultural teams, will prove to be a valuable asset for ABC, Inc.

If you have any questions, I can be reached at the number and e-mail address listed below.

Thank you for your time and consideration,

Susan Johnson
Operations Major—Supply Chain
Class of 20XX
Your University
Susan.johnson@university.edu
254.333.6565

You may notice on both of the examples of the cover letters that the statement prior to the text on qualifications is in bold print. This is to show emphasis and to draw the reader to these points.

Another form of written communication that should be sent is a Thank You letter. A thank you letter should be sent (as soon as possible) after every interaction, meeting, or chance association with an individual who can have an impact on your career. This is a wonderful way to gain notice by others who may have a hand in influencing your career.

This is an example of a thank you letter used after an interview.

Dear Ms. Smith;

Thank you for taking the time to discuss the financial analyst position at ABC, Inc., with me. After meeting with you and observing the company's operations, I am further convinced that my background and skills coincide well with your needs.

I really appreciate that you took so much time to acquaint me with the company. I feel I could learn a great deal from you and would certainly enjoy working with you. I truly believe my previous experience and my education have prepared me well for this position. I am very excited about this opportunity.

I look forward to hearing from you regarding your hiring decision. Again, thank you for your time and consideration.

Sincerely,

Betty Adams
Finance Major
Class of 20XX
Your University
Betty.Adams@university.edu
254.333.2332

Here is an example of a letter that would be sent to an alumnus in order to solicit an informational interview

January 26, 20XX

Ms. Whitley Jones
Director of Consumer Marketing
Jones & Simpson
254 Wilson Street
Raleigh, NC 26450

Dear Ms. Jones;

Professor John Wilson who teaches in the Marketing program at the Hankamer School of Business suggested I contact you regarding my career interest in marketing. He mentioned that you were one of his brightest students and went on to manage one of the top advertising firms in North Carolina.

He thought you would be a good person to talk with given my passion for the subject. As a junior at Hankamer, I am exploring different areas of the marketing field. My coursework has introduced me to a variety of options and has helped me develop my strategic and creative thinking. I would appreciate the opportunity to talk with you about your career path and would greatly appreciate your insight for students seeking an internship to better position their careers in the marketing field.

I would be pleased to come to your office, or give you a call at any time that is convenient for you. Thank you for taking time from your busy schedule, and I look forward to speaking with you.

Sincerely,

James Smith
Marketing Major
Class of 20XX
Your University
James.Smith@university.edu
254.333.6565

Any outreach can be tricky, but one that people struggle with is the dreaded post-interview follow up. This is not the thank you note that you need to send within 24 hours. This happens when you feel like you nailed the interview and you can't wait to hear back from the recruiter that you got the job. After the interview, you ask great closing questions and discuss the next step(s) in the interview process. They tell you they will get back to in the next few days, weeks, and or give you a specific day and that day passes and still no word from the recruiter. It's stressful to be waiting by the phone or constantly checking email for any news.

Most often these timelines are inaccurate at best. Realize that it's nothing personal and recruiters have a heavy workload. They are trying to hire for several positions, dealing with multiple hiring managers, and navigating deadlines. Most likely it may be just a timeline issue and they got too busy to get back to you within the specified time. Unfortunately, some recruiters will give you the "salesman's no" meaning they won't respond, but usually, it's a workload issue.

How can you as an interviewee get an update on your potential employment without being too annoying and desperate? In this case, the post-interview follow-up is recommended. If they have given you a specific date you may want to wait three to five business days after that date before sending this type of correspondence. If they did not give you a specific follow up timeline its recommended you wait 10 business days after the interview was conducted.

The goal of the post-interview follow-up is to let them know you are still interested in the position you interviewed for previously. It's a reminder to a busy recruiter or hiring manager you are still looking for communication. This type of communication will lead to a response and whether it is good or bad it provides closure.

Most recruiters will provide you with either a new updated timeline, a congratulations and let you know they are going to contact you soon with an offer, or that they have selected another candidate. Hopefully, it's an offer, but if not, you continue your career search. Here is the recommended outreach.

Month XX, 20XX

Mr. Slezak,

I wanted to touch base with you and tell you how excited I was about interviewing for the compliance position last week. It was really good to learn more about your career path, the company, and the position. I am excited about the potential of joining the Hewlett-Packard team.

After talking with you I feel that my professional background coupled with my skill sets and education make me the ideal candidate for this position. I have several years of compliance and auditing experience and a passion to work hard. I know I can be a valuable asset to your team. I am looking forward to learning as much as I can from you.

Please let me know if I can answer any possible questions. I look forward to hearing back from you and possibly joining your team. Thanks again for your time. If you need to reach me you can contact me via email at pat_neff@baylor.edu or you can reach me by phone at (254) 555-5555.

Sincerely,

Pat Neff
MIS Major
Class of 20XX
Your University
Pat_Neff@university.edu

Connecting and communicating are two foundations of your career management. You simply must practice these to realize your career potential. The more you practice the more capable you will become. If you are not as strong in these areas as you should be, just know the important thing is to begin and then push yourself to improve. Review your connections on a regular basis and make sure you are growing your professional contact list. You can do this.

© Rawpixel.com /Shutterstock.com

Chapter 7 Review Questions

1. The following statements about networking are all true:

   • You already know who you need to know.

   • You should communicate your interest to the people that care most about you.

   • Connect and build relationships and then ask non-threatening career-related questions.

   a) TRUE

   b) FALSE

2. When reaching out to an alumnus or networking contact for the very first time, what are some of the critical steps you should follow? Select three correct statements from the list below:

   a) Be professional and double check your e-mail for mistakes in spelling or grammar.

   b) Make sure and attach your resume in the first contact.

   c) Ask them to share their insights on their careers.

   d) If possible, establish a shared connection with your university, class, shared friends, or contacts.

   e) Ask them to help you identify opportunities in the company that might be a fit for you in the first contact.

3. What is the name of the book that was mentioned in this chapter with respect to networking and connecting?

   _____

   _____

4. When communicating with alumni, recruiters, hiring managers, and career contacts it is very important that you:

   a) Keep the correspondence professional.

   b) Be brief, specific and to the point, and try to always keep the document less than ½ page.

c) Check, re-check, and check again for misspelled words and proper grammar.

d) All of the above.

5. When you prepare for a phone interview you should:

a) Relax, it is informal and a routine preparation is not critical at this point.

b) Make sure you are in a quiet area that has good phone/cell support and smile when you speak.

c) Stand when you speak and make sure you have a copy of your resume and other job, company, and industry information at your fingertips.

d) All of the above

e) b and c only

f) None of the above

6. What is a side-by-side cover letter?

_____

_____

7. Connecting with others in your desired career field is a critical requirement to a successful career. When you initially reach out to connect with an alumnus or career contact, that you have not met, via e-mail or social media (LinkedIn) it is important to:

a) Be professional and respectful.

b) Acknowledge that the person is busy.

c) Ask for their insight regarding what it is like working in the industry and what advice they might have for a young college graduate entering the job market.

d) Ask permission to call them at their convenience.

e) Do not attach your resume or ask the contact to do anything until you have first established a relationship with the contact.

f) All of the above.

CHAPTER EIGHT

INTERVIEWING

© Keith Bell/Shutterstock.com

The interview is process is an evaluation by phone, video, or face to face by people who want to add capability to their organization. It may surprise you, but when you are interviewing, each and everything you do is being evaluated and critiqued. The first impression when you walk in the room may take all of 10–15 seconds as they assess your confidence

© Michal Kowalski/Shutterstock.com

and perceived capabilities through your handshake, eye contact, the way you carry yourself, your voice, expressions, the way you dress, and your overall presence and personality. If it is favorable that is great; if it is not, it will take major effort on your part to recover. This may seem unfair, but a first impression is just that - "a first impression."

When you prepare for your interview be sure to dress appropriately which means professionally. Unless you are interviewing for a fashion position, do not try and launch the latest fashion trends during your interview. Conservative dress is always the better choice in an interview setting. Men should wear a suit and tie and make sure their shoes are polished. Women should wear a suit as well with a conservative blouse and minimal accessories.

One word that should pop into your head when you think of interview is PREPARE. Effective preparation will set you apart from your peers and will significantly enhance your chances of receiving an offer. In chapter 3 we discussed the preparation required for understanding the industry, the company, and the role you are seeking. They are a crucial part of your interview preparation. Review this to understand the level of preparation you need in order to properly represent yourself as knowledgeable of and interested in the industry, the company, and the role you are seeking

INDUSTRY that you are interested in or that the company you are interested in does business

- ➤ Research the forecasts and trends of the revenue and profitability of the industry
- ➤ Research the number of major players and their associated market share
- ➤ Research expert opinions on the future outlook of the industry (Wall Street, Bloomberg, Industry Associations)
- ➤ Look at the major threats and opportunities to the industry
- ➤ Look at the industry with regard to its global footprint
- ➤ Check on major industry associations for recent issues and events
- ➤ Review the companies that are considered innovators in this industry
- ➤ Look at the Merger and Acquisition (M&A) activity over past 3 years within the industry

COMPANY you are interested in

- ➤ Look at the company's annual report (if a public company) and other published financial documents to gain a sense as to the future potential and forecasts of the company
- ➤ Research the company regarding the annual revenue dollars, the employee headcount, major locations, primary business units, senior leadership, and company culture
- ➤ Check the last 3 years of stock activity (if a public company)
- ➤ Read the last year of major press releases from the website
- ➤ Review the company's major competitors and their market share (this will be visible in their annual report if it is a public company)
- ➤ Understand the part that globalization plays in this company
- ➤ Understand the company's top customers and the percentage of business they provide to the company

➤ Understand the company's major products or services, and their associated strategy and performance (if published)

➤ Know the stated strategic mission and core values of the company (these will often be on the company's website and or in their annual report)

➤ Look at the legal and Merger and Acquisition (M&A) activity at this company in the last 3 to 5 years

ROLE or POSITION you are interested in

➤ Understand the primary requirements and qualification of the position and be able to speak to how you are qualified for each, then review your resume to insure it shows a strong fit

➤ Reach out to friends, family, professors, career management personnel, and alumni who can help you connect to individuals who have worked at the company or in the department or have during their professional career held the same or similar role. You can do this via LinkedIn or through the above mentioned contacts

➤ Research through the above bullet how your performance in this role would be evaluated

➤ Review the position via www.glassdoor.com where you can review the company and position as well as their interview process

➤ Uncover the salary norms for this type of position (inside and outside of this company) via www.glassdoor.com. This is an excellent resource for reviewing salaries for this type of position

➤ Understand what location you would be working from and the cost of living issues associated with that location

All three of these areas (Industry, Company, and Role) are critical preparation points for an interview. You should have a clear understanding of those three areas prior to your interview. If you actively prepare and can professionally address the questions inside those three sections (Industry, Company, and the Role you are seeking) from chapter 3, you will be well on your way to impressing your interviewers and setting yourself apart from the other applicants and interviewees. Another part of the preparation for an interview is learning as much as you can about the specific interview format, process, and structure of the company you are interviewing with. You can gain a reasonable amount of insight from www.glassdoor.com.

This website does an amazing job of capturing company information, salary information, employee information, and interview structure and interview question information. When you enter this website you can search on a multiple set of variables. The information that is captured on their site with respect to the interview and salary data is provided by individuals who access the site as a general course of their interaction with the platform. The salaries may be off a little based upon the honest input of those who provide it, but the interview experience is usually spot-on and accurate, at least from the recent interviewee's perspective.

The last part of the preparation is to have solid answers for every question that you are asked. While you will probably never know exactly what questions you will be asked you will still be able to prepare using the large set of questions that you "might" receive based upon the functional role you are interviewing for. These sets of practice questions are predominantly business related, but the general fit and negative behavioral questions will often be found regardless of the functional role for which you are interviewing. They are segmented by general functional interest for your review. If you are interviewing for a position that will require you to understand the functional areas we provided for you, be sure and review the questions and practice your answers until you are confident you can professionally represent your career potential.

© Mangostar/Shutterstock.com

General Behavioral Questions

1. What makes you a better fit for the job than other candidates we are interviewing?
2. What strengths will you bring to this position?
3. If selected for the job, what do you want to accomplish in the first three months?
4. Why did you choose our company over a competitor?
5. Why should we hire you?
6. Describe yourself in three adjectives.
7. What important trends do you see in our industry?
8. What is your motto in life?
9. What questions do you have for us?
10. What questions do you wished we would have asked?
11. What is the greatest challenge you have ever faced?
12. Tell me something about you that I will not discover from your resume.
13. What is the most significant accomplishment in your life?
14. What is the difference in a manager and a leader?
15. What is your management style—give an example?

16. What goals do you have in your career? And how do you plan to achieve these goals?

17. What is the hardest decision you ever had to make and what decisions are the most difficult for you?

18. How do you personally define success?

19. If there was one thing you could change in your life what would it be?

20. What motivates you? What have you accomplished that demonstrates your initiative?

21. Do you work well under pressure/stress? Give an example.

22. Tell me about some of your recent goals and what you did to achieve them.

23. What do you think are the most important characteristics and abilities a person must possess to be successful? How do you rate yourself in those areas?

24. What are your strongest skills?

25. Do you handle conflict well? Give me an example.

26. Have you ever had a conflict with a boss or professor? How did you resolve it?

27. What major problem have you had to deal with recently?

28. What would your enemies say about you?

29. If I were to ask one of your professors or a supervisor to describe you, what would he or she say?

30. How have you performed under pressure or under strict deadlines?

31. What motivates you?

32. Who is your role model?

33. Tell me about a recent crisis you handled.

Behavioral Marketing Questions

1. What do you feel are the most important issues facing the consumer products industry today? (you can substitute the industry you are interested in and applying to in order to be relevant)

2. Tell me about a time you launched a new product or process.

3. Describe your personal brand to me.

4. Give an example of a good advertising campaign you have seen recently. What made it so good?

5. Give an example of a bad advertising campaign you have seen recently. What made it so bad?

6. How would you decide how to advertise a new product and/or how to spend your marketing budget effectively?

7. Tell me about a time you demonstrated the most creativity.

8. Give an example of when you were customer focused.

9. Tell me about a time when you conducted some intense market research that had a strong impact on a strategic direction you choose.

10. Tell me about a time when you managed an outside vendor.

11. Describe a product you would market differently.

12. Give me an example when you sold something to someone that they did not want to buy.

13. You need more shelf space in a store, how do you convince the store manager to give it to you?

14. Give an example of an instance where you successfully introduced a new efficient and alternative spin on an old process.

15. You're the incoming Product Manager for your company's top product. You can only ask the outgoing manager three questions. What would they be?

16. Pick any developing country, how would you market our latest product to consumers in that country?

17. Tell me about any e-marketing or social media experience you have that would benefit our marketing department.

Behavioral Operations Questions

1. What was your most memorable operations leadership moment?
2. What was the largest project team you worked with, and what challenges did you face?
3. What is your idea of the ideal operations management team?
4. What project are you the most proud of?
5. Tell me about any cross-cultural or global team experience you have.
6. Have you worked on cross-functional teams with various Subject Matter Experts (SMEs)?
7. Tell me about a time when a boss or someone above you resisted an idea you had and how you were able to convince them to take a different course.
8. Give an example of a project that required an extraordinary amount of detail to complete.
9. Tell me about the most difficult negotiation you have been involved with.
10. What is the most difficult type of person for you to work with in a project team environment?
11. Tell me how you would react to a situation where there was more than one way to accomplish the same task, and other team members had ideas contrary to yours.

Technical Operations Questions

1. What do you understand about Supply Chain Management?
2. What is the "bullwhip effect" in supply chain, how does it affect the supply chain and how would you reduce it?
3. Explain the vendor rating process.
4. What are the risks in procurement how do you minimize these risks?

5. What is the difference between physical inventory and cycle counting and which process is better and why?

6. Explain consumption-based planning and demand-based planning, which is better and how.

7. How do you analyze inventory shrinkage?

8. What items of information are required in order to process a purchase requisition?

9. What are the pros and cons of a centralized purchasing function?

10. Define "supply chain."

11. What are the characteristics of an effective RFP (Request for Proposal)?

12. What is SAP? How is it related to databases? What is the basic concept?

13. What are the main objectives of a Project Manager?

14. Your three-month project is about to exceed the projected budget after the first month. What steps will you take to address the potential cost overrun?

15. What is "project float?"

16. What are the methods used for project estimation?

17. What metrics would you expect to use to determine the success of a project?

18. What analysis and modeling techniques do you use to translate business objectives into system requirements?

19. What is the difference between demand management and supply management?

20. Between the different types of contracts (blanket and fixed) in procurement, which type of contract should be used in what conditions?

21. What is in-transit inventory and how is it calculated and how do you monitor in-transit inventory levels?

Behavioral Finance Questions

1. Have you ever managed a budget, describe the process?
2. Tell me about the most challenging financial analysis you have been involved with.
3. Tell me about a situation that shows your analytical abilities.
4. Have you ever done analytical work that someone else took credit for? How did you feel?
5. What have you done in your past that qualifies you for a position in finance?
6. Do you currently have your own portfolio? What have you learned from your gains and losses?
7. What are your strength areas in finance?
8. Give an example of a previous project that required an extraordinary amount of detail to complete.
9. Tell me about a financial model you have created.
10. Describe an analytical process you created that have had an impact on a business or project.
11. Describe a financial project you participated in that was ambiguous at the start and how you handled it.

Technical Finance Questions

1. How do I find a WACC?
2. What ratios do you think are the most important to valuing a company and why?
3. How does depreciation affect the three financial statements?
4. What is the difference between enterprise value multiples and P/E multiples?
5. Describe how the three main financial statements flow together.
6. ABC Company's net income is 200 million. How do I compute their cash flow?
7. What is working capital?

8. What major factors drive mergers and acquisitions?

9. Explain DCF to me as you would a relative who does not know finance.

10. How would you explain a credit spread?

11. How do you measure Return on Invested Capital?

12. Define free cash flow.

13. Define EVA.

14. What is convexity?

15. What kind of multiples do you look at when you value stock?

16. What is Beta?

17. What is the problem of using terminal value?

18. What is the difference between default and prepayment risk?

19. Are you better off using implied standard deviation or historical standard deviation to forecast volatility? Why?

20. When do companies typically buy back stock?

21. Why would a company issue stock rather than debt to finance its operations?

22. What are the four methods to value a company? Explain the pros/cons of each?

23. What are the procedures or processes involved in the preparation for an audit?

24. Tell us about specific profitability models used for forecasting, business casing, and ad hoc analyses you have developed and maintained for a specific project.

25. Which is better for a firm, debt or equity financing?

26. Which is a better indication of firm's growth? Balance sheet or income of statements?

27. Differentiate between Investment Banking and Private Equity.

28. What would you look at to estimate the overall financial health of a company?

29. Explain the terms: fixed cost, variable cost, and marginal cost.

30. How does goodwill affect the net economy of a firm?

Negative-Style Behavioral Questions

1. What is the worst mistake you have ever made at work? What did you learn?

2. What are your weaknesses? Give me an example of three?

3. Tell me about a time you failed at something.

4. If hired, what area would you need to improve on in the first three months?

5. Tell me about a time when your boss was angry with you.

6. If you were made CEO of this company what would you change?

7. Describe your worst job.

8. Have you ever made a mistake with a customer? How did they react?

9. Describe a situation where you got "in over your head at work."

10. At what time in your life have you been the most discouraged?

11. When have you let others or yourself down?

12. Tell me about time when you were on a team and another team member did not like you.

13. Give me an example of a difficult person for you to get along with.

14. What did you dislike about your previous job?

15. If I invited you to be my friend on Facebook, what negative things would I see on your page?

16. What bad habits do you have?

As you read through the questions, you may wonder how are you supposed to know if the answers you come up with for these questions are the correct ones or for that matter what is the company really looking for. You may even ask yourself why would a company ask these types of questions? In addition, what are they really looking for? Most behavioral questions are asked in order to determine more about "who you really are" and how well will you fit in their organization.

© CandyBox Images/Shutterstock.com

One of the best books that addresses the questions you might have on behavioral interviews is *How to Interview Like a Top MBA* by Dr. Shel Leanne. The contents of the book are very applicable to anyone who is interviewing for a professional position. The early chapters of this book deal with how to make a great impression during an interview, how to prepare and make the most of an interview. The remaining balance of the book goes into detail with approximately 100 questions. The book speaks to the basis of those questions, why an employer would ask them, and some background and analysis on the answers. This book should be part of your personal career management program.

When you are interviewing you will be asked about prior performance and you will also be asked to provide examples that will help substantiate your credibility. If you are asked about your ability to deal with stress, ambiguity, deadlines, multiple commitments, unhappy customers, etc. how will you respond? A recommended strategy is to practice those types of questions by answering in a specific format or structure in order to enhance your ability to have a solid and credible answer. Recruiters and Human Resource professionals are all very familiar with the technique of formatting answers called STAR. This has been around for a number of years and stands for Situation, Task, Action, and Results.

It is not uncommon for an interviewer to ask someone a question and ask them to answer in a STAR format . . . or to downgrade a person's potential interview ranking if they do not answer in a STAR format. The STAR format allows you to package your answers to behavioral questions in a manner that helps you recall the events and past performances in order to aid in the credibility of your answers. The S (Situation) is simply a quick description or overview of the situation or context in which the story you are about to relate was occurring. The T (Task) provides an overview of the challenge you faced and the issue you needed to resolve. The A (Action) describes the actions you took to resolve the challenge and should display desired transferable skill sets. And the R (Results) provides the impact and the results of your efforts. The Results are the most important element of your STAR story and should include the qualitative as well as quantitative impacts, including recognition, you achieved. When you tell a STAR story you need to think in terms of impactful results and how this story shows a strong fit for the requirements of the role you are seeking.

Taking one of the general behavioral questions you reviewed on the previous pages:

#21. Do you work well under pressure/stress? Give an example.

The worksheet in the example can help you prepare for this question. It has already been completed to demonstrate how to best utilize it.

STAR STORY WORKSHEET

STAR Story Name: "Weekend to Remember"

(use names or titles in your story that will help you remember the story)

Above story could be used for other interview topics in the following areas:

Project management	Leadership
Teamwork	Market Assessment

Situation: (General context—Who, What, Where, situation, and history of problem)— complete within 30 seconds

I was part of a four-person project team from our senior-level capstone class where we met with local businesses over the semester and provided consulting and research support for their business. The final assignment of the class was a presentation or our recommendations to the business leaders of the company.

Task: (Nature of challenge to overcome, what is required to resolve the issue, your role, difficulty level, scope, how it came to your desk)—complete within 30 seconds

My role was to provide a market assessment for their new product as well as discuss the potential cannibalization from this product of their main product revenue generator. My role was to provide the marketing research and support for this task.

Action: (How did you solve the problem: your actions performed to address the specific topics above)—complete within 30 seconds

The weekend before the assignment was due; the teammate who was responsible for compiling the input from each member the group into a cohesive PowerPoint presentation was in a serious accident and was hospitalized. I volunteered to build the presentation as well as complete her segment which included a financial roll-up of our recommendations. I worked nonstop through the weekend with less than 4 hours of sleep between

Friday and Monday morning. I finished the presentation and the financial roll-up in the early hours of Monday morning and with my other two remaining teammates we practiced the presentation which was presented at 10 am Monday.

Results: (Personal, business, or professional impact, recognition received)—complete within 30 seconds

The company praised the recommendations and complimented our team on our efforts and content. After the presentation, I was approached by their director of marketing who had utilized his in-house resources to build a market assessment. He stated that he was very impressed with my recommendation and felt the overall team recommendation was far better than he expected from a group of college students with little to no industry experience. He was so impressed that he offered me a position with the company upon graduation.

> * As you can see, this story would allow you to speak genuinely about an accomplishment that addresses several questions that you might get in an interview setting. Besides the question "do you work well under pressure/stress . . . and give an example" you could also use this STAR story for several other topics such as Project Management, Leadership, Teamwork, and Market Assessment.

> * We recommend that each student have at least four and as many as eight STAR stories at your disposal. You may say "why so many?" The answer to that is you need a STAR story for each major requirement of the role that you are seeking. If you look at the internship or job description for the role you seek you will see several major requirements or qualifications. You should prepare (and practice) a STAR story for each. You should also have a STAR story for any likely general fit behavioral questions. Like the one we just answered "do you work well under pressure/stress."

Below is a list of possible topics you should create STAR stories to address:

- Team building
- Leadership
- Ambiguity
- Sales Skills
- Delegation
- Organization Skills
- Communication Skills
- Greatest Weakness/Strength
- Decision Making
- Management Skills
- Showing Initiative
- Problem Solving
- Attitude/Commitment
- Strategic Thinking
- Motivating Others
- Adapting to Change
- Handling Pressure/Stress

Next is a simple STAR story summary worksheet that allows you to list the internship or job title you are seeking and then the four major requirements of the role. Next to that set of four boxes is your respective STAR story for each one. You do not have to insert the full requirement or qualification in the summary box, just enough so you are clear on the requirement. The same goes for the STAR story, you can input the name of your STAR story if you prefer. You may use the same STAR story for multiple requirements if there is a common fit. The work sheet lists two internship or job titles, but you can copy this and make it for as many as you need.

	Internship and Job STAR Match Worksheet			
Internship / Job Title	Major Internship or Job Requirements		STAR stories that Support Requirements	
#1				
#2				

One area within the Interview section that you need to be aware of is the need to avoid "negative selling." Negative selling is when you answer a question with an unsolicited negative comment about yourself. Here are some examples:

Question—Tell me about a time you led a group and moved them to a positive outcome.

Answer—I have not really led a group before but I know I have the capability to be a great leader.

Surely you have led something in your entire career . . . it is much better to give the recruiter a sense that you can move others to a positive outcome by providing a good STAR story for example or a general statement that shows you have "potential."

Question—Can you give me an example of your finance skills?

Answer—I actually did not major in Finance, but I did take several classes in Finance and made A's.

You could have answered "I completed ABC project in finance and made an . . ." or "I worked on a project with my classmates to review the financial health of a local company and received an A." The main point is you did not have to say you did not major in finance. This is simply you giving the recruiter an unsolicited negative attribute on yourself. Don't do it. They did not ask you if you majored in Finance. An interviewer/ recruiter is looking specifically for negatives. You do not have to provide any extra. Do not be dishonest, but also do not provide negatives on yourself unless specifically asked to do so.

Another tip for you when you are interviewing is to stay focused on the position you are interviewing for when you are in an interview setting. Sometimes a student who was performing well during an interview and was a strong functional fit based on skills and past performance to the role and also appeared to be a strong fit culturally to the department can completely lose the interview simply by not focusing on the job at hand. The "train came off the track", if you will allow me that analogy, when the interviewer asked about long-term career interests. One student said he wanted to gain a few years of experience and then open up his own business; another student said she needed to build their resume with a couple of years working for a respected company before they applied to grad school: and another student said they felt they could do this job, but really wanted a position in another department and interviewing for. felt this was the best way to get in the door.

You can imagine that the recruiter lost interest almost immediately. The recruiter, hiring manager, human resource professional, and even the company you are interviewing with wants to believe that you want to work and dedicate yourself to the role you are interviewing for. It is likely you really do not know what you want to do until you have more professional work experience. So if asked about your interest it should be the job or internship you are interviewing for at that time, and if asked about your long-term career interests it is advisable to answer that, based on your research so far, you would love to be in a similar functional role, but with greater challenges and responsibility.

Another area that you may encounter in an interview is a "case" interview. This is very different from a behavioral or technical-type interview. In a case interview, the interviewer will provide you with a set of circumstances and ask you for a solution. There are numerous excellent books on how to effectively prepare for a case interview. Two are: *Case in Point— Complete Case Interview Preparation* by Marc P. Cosentino (www.casequestions.com) and *Crack the Case—How to Conquer Your Case Interviews* by David Ohrvall (www.mbacase.com).

Another source for practicing and preparing for a case interview is www.consultingcase101.com. On this website you can search cases by company, by industry, and by functional expertise.

There are a few things you should know about a case interview. While the interviewer would be very impressed if you provide the exact answer for the case analysis, they are primarily looking for how you process the case. Do you ask solid questions (which you should after you are given the case), are you clear what the interviewer is looking for and for the type of solution for which the case is looking? It is very easy to get lost in the weeds or spend your precious case analysis time chasing issues that have no bearing or relevance on the case (and especially the type of solution that the interviewer is seeking). Oftentimes you will be given a brief amount of time to solve the case, without the aid of a calculator or internet access and the interviewer is looking for how you process the analytics as well as the strategy aspects.

Two general types of cases are given to students.

1. Very broad and completely disconnected from the company or functional role—cases such as:

   How many disposable diapers are consumed in the US in one year?

   How many golf balls will fit into a 747?

   How many trucks of dirt will it take to move Mt. Fuji?

These cause you to scratch your head with respect to "who cares," but just know the interviewer is looking to see how you function with such an off-the-wall question. If you roll your eyes and say "I don't know" they know you probably are not big on curiosity, problem solving, and dealing with ambiguity. If on the other hand you say: "you know, I have never thought of that question before, but . . . if there are approximately 310 million people in the US and X number of that are between the ages of Y and Z and of those children a percentage (%) would use disposable diapers and of those that use disposable diapers, I would estimate they would use an approximate number of diapers a day multiplied by 365 days a year and this would equal approximately X disposable diapers consumed in a year." The precision of the answer is not nearly important as how you approach and attack the problem. Something that will help you with this type of cases and others like it is to look at the structure of what is required; it is acceptable to make assumptions if they are reasonable. Afterall, you have probably never measured a golf ball or the interior of a 747, so assumptions are fine.

The one thing you can always control is your attitude. Go at the case interview with the right attitude and you will do well the majority of time.

2. More specific to the industry, company, and your role and the interviewer will be looking to evaluate and validate your analytical and business judgment skills.

Common Case Interview Scenarios that fall into this category tend to address the functional areas of your role, including: strategy, marketing, finance, and on occasion in IT and Human Resources. It is recommended that you practice multiple scenarios in your area of interest, plus stretch out into other disciplines. Each of the scenarios listed below can be inside the employer's industry or purposely from another industry.

Marketing Scenarios	Strategy Scenarios	Finance Scenarios
New Product Launch	Mergers & Acquisitions	Reducing Costs
New Market Entry	Company Turnaround	Profitability Analysis
Market Share Decline		
Pricing Strategy	**Human Resources**	**Information Technology**
Competitive Response	Considerations of Downsizing	New System Implementation
Market Segmentation	Staff Retention Strategy	Project Cost Estimations
Increasing Sales	Recruitment Strategy	

You can find cases to practice via the www.consultingcase101.com website. If you are looking at consulting, financial analysis with a large firm or a marketing, strategy, or business development role, you may be given a case during an interview. You should check www.glassdoor.com for interview techniques and tactics. You should also check the company's website in the student career section, as they often tell students what to expect and how to prepare (even giving them cases to practice). Practice at least ten cases for each case you think you will receive in an interview and more if at all possible.

Even though case interviews are not as common as behavioral interviews you should practice them as a part of your interview preparation. Practicing a case interview will help you gain a sense for solving complex problems without all the critical information at your fingertips. It will give you a bigger perspective for the issues the company will face and it will help you think about problems and solutions at a higher level.

One last point you should be aware of when it comes to having a successful interview experience is having great questions ready for your interviewer. You need to have questions prepared in advance so you can take advantage of this opportunity. Here are a few questions that may help you if you are struggling to come up with something:

1. What do you enjoy most about working for the company?
2. If you could change one thing about how the company is run what would that be?
3. What do you think makes this company unique in the marketplace?

These questions will buy you a little time, but you really need to follow up one of these "general questions" with something more strategic. As part of your interview preparation, you should have reviewed the company's and the industry's latest news and press releases. You should extract from the current activities of the company and the industry important points so that you can ask questions about strategy, market share, market positioning, competitive advantages, business trends, impact from recent mergers and acquisitions, technical advantages, quality concerns, customer trends, government involvement, global competitiveness, and recent innovative products or services. Asking great questions shows the interviewer you are definitely interested in the company and that you bring a mindset that looks beyond just your functional role. You care about the bigger picture and are invested in an awareness that sets you apart from your peers.

When it comes to interviews this is a defining moment for you. You have worked so hard to position yourself for this opportunity. It would be a shame to have a chance like this and simply not prepare effectively. You never know what interview and what opportunity will be the one that becomes the door-opener to your career.

If you prepare as outlined in this chapter you will be able to represent yourself in a manner that can lead to an offer. Take advantage of every opportunity to interview as you will become more polished and professional with each round of interviews. In addition, push yourself, do not take shortcuts and prepare for each opportunity so that when you leave the interview you have set a standard by which all other applicants will be measured. You can do it.

LOOK YOUR BEST
PROFESSIONAL DRESS FOR MEN

- Conservative two-piece fitted suit in subdued colors
- Long-sleeve shirt in light color or conservative pattern
- Simple tie with a slight pop of color
- Match your belt with your shoes in color. Black is suggested for interviews
- Keep jewelry to a minimum: wristwatch and wedding ring at most
- Dark-colored socks with dress shoes
- All clothing should be wrinkle-free

DON'T FORGET:
Clean-shaven or well-groomed facial hair and clean, trimmed nails

Image © Whitney Kent. Reprinted by permission

BAYLOR
UNIVERSITY
HANKAMER SCHOOL OF BUSINESS
Career Management

LOOK YOUR BEST
PROFESSIONAL DRESS FOR WOMEN

- Fitted (not snug) 2-piece suit in subdued colors
- Skirt no more than 2 inches above the knee or hemmed pants
- Modest blouse in contrasting color
- Simple jewelry
- Medium height, closed-toe heel in matching color
- Plain purse or attaché
- All clothing should be wrinkle-free

DON'T FORGET:
Polished hair, natural makeup & manicured nails in light or natural color

Image © Whitney Kent. Reprinted by permission.

BAYLOR
UNIVERSITY
HANKAMER SCHOOL OF BUSINESS
Career Management

Interview Strategy Tips

- Become the Ideal Candidate and Speak to the Job Description/Position
- Prepare! Prepare! Prepare! Use the 3 Whys & STAR Stories
- Don't be Afraid to Brag on Yourself
- Dress for Success
- Show Energy & Enthusiasm
- Bring a Padfolio, with Resumes, Notes, and Room to Take Notes
- Immediately Write and Send Thank You Notes! (Personalize Them)
- When Appropriate, Follow Up

Chapter 8 Review Questions

1. When preparing for an interview, what are at least three things you need to research about the industry you are interested in?

    a) _____

    b) _____

    c) _____

2. When preparing for an interview, what are at least three things you need to research about the company you are interested in?

    a) _____

    b) _____

    c) _____

3. When preparing for an interview, what are at least three things you need to research about the job or internship that you are applying for?

    a) _____

    b) _____

    c) _____

4. To have the greatest chance for success in an interview you need to be able to answer three critical questions. Answer the questions below for your most desired role, which is available within your favorite company (employer), which also participates in your industry of interest.

    a) Why do you think you are our best choice for this job or internship? _____

    _____

    _____

b) Why do you think this company is a great fit for you?

_____

_____

c) Why is this industry attractive to you? _____

_____

_____

_____

5. Select 6 questions from the list of 33 General Behavioral
   Questions in Chapter 8 and answer them below.
   Remember your answers need to be compelling and
   provide positive reinforcement for a recruiter looking at
   you as their next potential employee.

   a) _____

   _____

   b) _____

   _____

   c) _____

   _____

   d) _____

   _____

   e) _____

   _____

   f) _____

   _____

6. What is STAR? _____

   _____

7. Answer the following question in STAR format. We have reviewed your resume and application and we have other applicants with quite a bit more experience than you. **Specifically**, why should we hire you?

S = _____

_____

T = _____

_____

A = _____

_____

R = _____

_____

8. What letter is the most important in STAR and…..Why?

a) What letter is most important = _____

b) Why = _____

CHAPTER NINE

THE OFFER AND NEGOTIATIONS

© Andy Dean Photography/Shutterstock.com

You worked very hard and felt like the interview went amazingly well. As you are leaving the interview, you ask the Human Resources (HR) representative when you might hear regarding the hiring decision. The person tells you that you should hear something within a week or so. You send thank you notes by email to each of the individuals you met with during the interview. You also send a request to connect with the interviewers via LinkedIn. You then begin that all too fun, character-building, emotional roller coaster ride called "waiting." There are several things you will learn as you wait. One of those is that if the company tells you they will get back with you in a week or so, it is usually two weeks or more.

Another thing you will learn is the need to aggressively and actively continue hunting for another opportunity for which you are a strong fit. Too many students put all of their hopes and dreams into one interview with one company and then wait for three to four weeks to find out they were not the person selected for the role. Sadly, you just lost nearly a month of your job hunt, not to mention emotional capital, as you feel like you are starting over from the beginning. You should continue to actively hunt for other positions that you are interested in and by all means apply and aggressively research, practice, and position yourself for success. There is an old saying, "hope for the best, but plan for the worst". Be prepared for rejection, for non-responses to your application, for non-returned emails and phone calls. Understand that rejection is part of the career process and although it is not fun, learn from it and let it fuel you to work harder to realize your career dreams.

Now, back to the first paragraph regarding the interview; you finally receive a call from the recruiter and they tell you they are excited to offer you a position at $50,000 (maybe it is $30,000 or maybe it is $90,000, whatever is appropriate for your degree, major and experience level). You are ecstatic about the call, but you did your research on the salary and you were honestly expecting more. What do you do?

First, you should have actively researched the position as we discussed in earlier chapters, and part of that research would have given you an average or approximate salary range for the position you applied to and for which you are a strong fit. We talked previously about www.glassdoor.com and how you can search for interview structure and company reviews. You can also search salaries for general internship and job positions and even salaries for the specific position within the company to which you are applying and interviewing. Other websites that are very helpful when it comes to salary research are: www.beyond. com, www.salary.com, and www.payscale.com. All these websites give you a chance to search by company or by functional role with respect to gaining insight into salary information. You should research and utilize them all and keep a spreadsheet or list of what you find. You should also communicate with your university career professional staff to research the average salary that students are receiving for your respective major upon graduation. You want to be as knowledgeable as possible regarding the compensation available for your role.

You should also understand that there is more to compensation than a base salary. There may be a sign-on bonus for the position, which means that the company will pay you additional dollars for coming to work for them in addition to your base salary. Normally, when you receive a sign-on bonus, you receive a portion of the amount in your first check and the balance after 90 days. Most companies will pay sign-on bonuses to secure talent in a competitive job market and then do not pay sign-on bonuses when there is light demand for hiring with many candidates available for the role. So depending on the recruiting competitiveness of the role that you are seeking, you might be looking at a nice sign-on bonus.

There may also be relocation compensation, bonuses (monthly, quarterly, or annual) tied to your performance or the company's performance or a hybrid of both. There may also be other incentives that the company provides that makes this company more attractive to you than other companies. It could be the amount of money the company contributes to your savings program, health, dental, optical, life insurance, educational assistance, in-house services such as a gym or gym membership, dry-cleaning, cafeteria, parking, and many more.

When you research the company, you will typically not have visibility on all of these incentives, but they will be described to you when you see the formal offer. If you have any questions about the offer that have not been fully satisfied by your discussion with the recruiter, wait until you receive, and review, the formal hard copy offer to question them further. When you receive the offer, review it in detail and then connect with the HR or recruiting contact for clarification and take notes on their answers.

Now, back to the phone call that contains your verbal offer from the recruiter: you are excited, your head is spinning, and you want to say "yes," but you know you should take some time to fully consider the offer and the opportunity. So the call comes in, they make the offer . . . now what do you do? Well, first and foremost, how you respond to the call is always up to you and is, and should be, based on your personal circumstances.

The company

"Hi, this is Jane Smith and I am the Human Resource Manager for ABC Company and we are pleased to offer you a job as a business development associate at an annual salary of $50,000."

Your response

"Thank you very much for the offer and I am very excited about being a part of the company. Ms. Smith, even though the salary is secondary compared to the satisfaction of the position, I wonder if the company has any flexibility with the offer amount."

The company

Option A: "We think our salary offer is very competitive. What were you looking for?"

Your response

"I know that ABC Company is a highly regarded firm, but I was hoping for a salary of $55,000.

The company

"Why do you feel $55,000 is appropriate?"

Your response

"The average base salary for this past year, for students who graduated with a Bachelor's in Business Administration and majoring in Management was $55,000. I wanted to at least be at the average for my degree." (Assuming this is an accurate representation of the facts for your situation . . . also, this is why you need to do your research on the salary and placement data at your university.)

Most employers have a built-in range for salary offers and they typically do not start at the top when they make an offer. The strategy behind your response is to never give the employer an ultimatum or to in anyway threaten to "not accept" their offer if it does not meet your expectations. Instead, you give the recruiter a chance to play the "good guy or gal" and provide an increase that is reasonable. For most new college hires (Undergrad and Graduate) there is a potential increase in the majority of salary offerings from 5 to 10% and this level of increase is often considered realistic and reasonable. Also . . . there is a solid statistic that I have seen which shows that there is a 100% chance you will not get an increase in your base salary if you do not ask for it. Ask for more if you need it, but just be aware that you will have more success with something that is reasonable than something that is not.

Here is another viewpoint on this example:

The company

"Hi, this is Jane Smith and I am the Human Resource Manager for ABC Company and we are pleased to offer you a job as a business development associate at an annual salary of $50,000."

Your response

"Thank you very much for the offer and I am very excited about being a part of the company. Ms. Smith, even though the salary is secondary compared to the satisfaction of the position, I wonder if the company has any flexibility with the offer amount."

The company

Option B: "I am sorry, but the salary offer is firm."

Your response

"I can appreciate that and even though I was hoping for additional compensation I will accept your offer."

This is, of course, if you want to accept the offer. If you believe you should be paid a higher amount and you have done your research and it backs this up . . . and . . . you have other opportunities that are at least as interesting as this one, then say:

"I greatly appreciate the offer and would love to be a part of the company, but I was hoping for a base salary of $XYZ. If you think there is potential for the company to meet that amount I would be very interested in a position."

You should always ask for time to evaluate the offer. In most instances you will be given a reasonable amount of time, but smart recruiters know the more time that you are given, the greater the chance they will lose you if you have been interviewing with other firms. Once you have their offer you now have extra confidence that you have a solid backup plan and you can be more aggressive with other opportunities. You would also use the first company's offer as your floor and anything above that would be perceived as a better option assuming the roles and opportunities are similar. You have to be careful with this way of thinking however, and that is why research on the salary and offer package of the company is so important. Do not compare simply dollars to dollars on the separate opportunities. Consider the career growth potential, the industry status, the company ranking and reputation, and the people you will be working with as that would have greater emphasis than just a few thousand dollars in difference.

Other Potential Negotiation Topics

1. DOUBLE MAJOR OR DUAL DEGREE STUDENT - Additional degrees, certifications, and academic rigor above and beyond your peers could give you an advantage in the negotiations.

Some students have held full time jobs while in college or even fully supported themselves through college without any assistance from parents, friends, or family.

2. SPECIALIZED MAJOR - You may be in an elite group of students or in a specialized major. That major may give you the exact transferable skills that are hard to find and extremely desirable to the recruiter. You may have been selected into an elite group of students and achieved significant academic results, possibly even a 4.0. Case competition teams or consulting teams give you the student the ability to prove to employers through experience(s) that you deserve a higher initial starting salary as well.

3. RELOCATION & COST OF LIVING CONCERNS - Geographic issues may be hindering you or cause you to rethink the compensation package of the job offer. Certain parts of the US can be far more expensive than other parts of the country. Texas for instance has a much cheaper cost of living than California or New York. You must consider all the variables. The cost may be higher based on state income tax, transportation costs, food costs, home values and property taxes. Cost of living can create significant financial struggles if you are not aware of what you are getting into when you accept your offer. We suggest a few of the following tools that will help you analyze the cost of living:

http://money.cnn.com/calculator/pf/cost-of-living/index.html

https://www.payscale.com/cost-of-living-calculator

https://www.bestplaces.net/cost-of-living/

These tools will help you get an idea of the true cost exchange of living in that city. A $55,000 offer in Dallas, Texas may be more lucrative than a $72,000 offer in New York in the context of take home pay or disposable income.

New graduates, young professionals, and seasoned veterans alike need to be prepared to answer this question. You need to do your research and make sure you are prepared. It would be incredibly embarrassing to be on the phone with a recruiter and be caught off-guard, and say something like "I just think I am worth it" or "I need the money." Be ready to present a solid, justifiable stance on why you deserve more money.

Now when you are in the process of negotiating with your future employer you are equipped to handle those difficult questions like things you "Why are you worth more money" or "What exactly are you looking for and why? You can easily articulate your value in the open market. Know your value and don't sell yourself short.

Potentially, the single most important factor in your success and career growth is the mentor you will be working for or with. If you are fortunate enough to have the opportunity to work for someone you respect and who is also respected in their field AND they like you and also have an excellent track record in developing subordinates for greater responsibilities . . . then you have just hit the career jackpot. This employment situation would be much preferred over another employment situation with similarly ranked companies even if the other company was paying you slightly more in base salary. It is so easy to get caught up in the starting salary game, when in reality the difference is not your first job, role and position, but your second and third as this is where you will be positioning yourself for the next 5–10 years. A few thousand dollars in year one looks great for the first year, but pales quickly by the earnings potential when you are in a more strategic company or with a person who cares about your career growth.

Look at the total offer and the bigger picture. Do not sell yourself short in earnings potential and realize that although the first job is very important you are developing your career for the long term.

Negotiations are often perceived as two people arm wrestling or playing high stakes poker, winner takes all. In reality, the best negotiations are where there are two winners, you and the person you are negotiating with. That is why you need to give the recruiter, HR representative, or hiring manager an opportunity to know what you are looking for when they are making an offer. Give them an out or chance to gracefully decline without damaging the relationship. Do not propose things with ultimatums of unreasonable compensation or deadlines.

One of the reasons for this is that the industry you end up working in is not nearly as large as it seems and you will be surprised with the people you meet along the way. The person you work for in your first job may be a peer in your second or third, the recruiter that hires you may end up at a competitor and three years later be recruiting you again. It is much better to build human capital versus tearing it down by burning bridges. Always be professional and honest and it will bode well for you in the future. You will not make it through a 10–20–30-year career without some tense or highly charged business disagreements, but if you keep those disagreements professional you will likely keep the doors open with respect to the relationship. Avoid personal attacks because you never know whose paths you will cross and it is better to build allies than enemies.

When you research an opportunity and based on that analysis, ask for something that you and others in the industry would consider fair, and in a professional and non-threatening manner, there is a better than average chance it will work out. In our earlier example of the company offer and the counteroffer, there is a spirit of cooperation in the dialog. There is also a respectful and professional tone and that will go a long way in helping your point of discussion to be considered. In the ten plus years we have followed this course of action with our students those students who have asked for a reasonable increase have received the increase or some type of additional compensation or incentive at least 85% of the time.

If the recruiter says that they cannot meet your increased salary proposal you could end the conversation with, "Thank you for trying and I will accept your offer," or you might say, "I appreciate your consideration to improve the salary however, since that is not an option, would you by chance have flexibility with a sign-on bonus?" Remember you should have already checked to see if they have a recent history on paying sign-on bonuses for this role. Oftentimes, the base salary may be fixed for an entry level hire and they do not want to have multiple new hires with a wide range of salaries (even if they are within the pay range). Providing a sign-on bonus does two things: (1) it allows the new hire to receive additional compensation that incentivizes them to accept the offer and (2) it does not change the base salary structure within the company and this creates an easier administrative situation. The sign-on bonus is also a one-time event and does not repeat itself the following year.

After you accept the offer you will be given a start date. It is important that you try and meet the company's start date as that is the day they will typically have new employee orientation and training. Some things may come up and most companies are considerate in how they work with their new hires, but just be sensitive to the start date and the onboarding process that exists with the company.

You successfully navigated and positioned yourself through the application and interview process. Your efforts were rewarded with an offer. You have also negotiated a reasonable increase in your starting salary. Life is GREAT.

Now let us get to work and start earning your pay.

© Stephen Coburn/Shutterstock.com

Chapter 9 Review Questions

1. Which of the following are career tools that can help you assess the salary range for the role you are seeking when you graduate.

   a) www.glassdoor.com

   b) www.salary.com

   c) www.whatareyougoingtopaymedude.com

   d) www.beyond.com

   e) a, b, and d

   f) b and c

2. You are a new college graduate and you have just received a job offer from the Fortune 500 company that you are most excited about. You are happy with the offer for the most part, but would like to see an increase in salary. Your best option or options from the list below would be:

   a) Tell the recruiter you are unhappy with the offer and make a counter offer on your own before the recruiter has an opportunity to respond.

   b) Thank them for the offer and then ask if they have any flexibility on the salary.

   c) Research the position and assess the approximate new hire salaries and if your amount is within 5 percent of the initial offer use that amount when asked by the recruiter what you would like to see as a salary. On an average you stand a good chance of getting it.

   d) All the above

   e) b and c

   f) None of the above

3. The best attitude for you to have with your first professional job offer is to create a win–win for both parties.

   a) True

   b) False

4. Starting salaries are very important, but the opportunity, career potential, and career growth are more important.

   a) True

   b) False

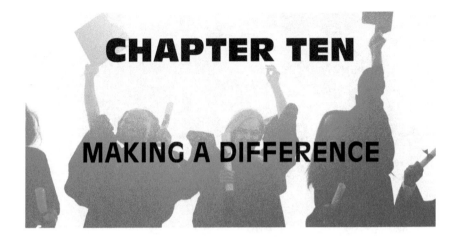

CHAPTER TEN

MAKING A DIFFERENCE

YOUR NEW CAREER

© RTimages/Shutterstock.com

C ongratulations, you are ready to start your first day on your new job. This will no doubt be an exciting experience for you. We want that excitement to continue long into your career. We also want the excitement to continue for your employer and ideally we want you to be one of the employees that establish a performance standard that all other great employees are measured against.

© dotshock/Shutterstock.com

When you start your first new job, one thing that will help you stay connected to your supervisor and insure that you are in sync with the department goals and objectives is to prepare a brief weekly report. This appears like extra work for you and it could even potentially be a vehicle to show you are not being productive. However, you shouldn't look at this small administrative task as extra work or a possible red flag of lack of productivity.

This could be one of the most important things you do at the end of each week. Your supervisor will know what you are working on and because of this (and the fact you are doing it voluntarily) he/she will know you are a results-driven individual and someone who can be counted on to get things done. You will be very surprised how just doing a half page to a page weekly update on your major activities will assist your career. It will keep you engaged and connected and that is one of the most valuable benefits of the weekly report. Ideally, it would include the project name, due date, status, and any notes or comments regarding the progress or lack thereof.

You may or may not know this, but most employees leave their company not because of pay, work conditions, long commute, pressure, or stress, but because they feel unappreciated. They believe they are disconnected from the overall goals and objectives of their department and the company, and they very often believe their boss or immediate supervisor is not really interested in what they are doing. In short, they feel they are just occupying space for eight hours a day to get a paycheck.

Reality alert . . . If you feel unappreciated in your job, take a look in the mirror as there is a high probability you expect others to be fully aware of your efforts and the potential impact you make on a daily basis. The truth is your boss or immediate supervisor is normally very busy with their own action items and they assume you are doing your best to meet your commitments. They would be surprised to know that you feel unappreciated. All of this misunderstanding and miscommunication can be resolved with something as simple as a brief weekly report. Most bosses will appreciate the fact you provide this and if there is something you have on your list that they are not aware of or familiar with, they will ask questions to become informed. Because of this the two of you can work together to realign your priorities or major projects if necessary.

You want to do a great job and you will do your very best with respect to performance, but there are often some subtle things you can do to enhance the likelihood you are on the company's fast-track list. You want to be one of the employees that are looked to when decisions are being made to distribute additional responsibility or projects. Note, that when you are on the receiving end of additional responsibility or projects, you should consider this an interview for potential promotion. Do not take the added responsibility or opportunity lightly.

Here are some quick tips:

- Be early and stay late! At least 15 minutes early and 15 minutes after normal quitting time . . . It does make a difference.
- Do not take excessive breaks.
- Do not make a habit of calling in sick unless you are deathly ill/contagious with the plague. Every boss or seasoned manager recognizes the Monday flu.
- Do not make a habit of showing up late to work or to any scheduled meetings.

- Do not make excuses . . . ever! Just be the person that always completes their assignments. This will be noticed and will heighten your chances of being successful.

- Be open minded and willing to volunteer for tasks, assignments, and projects. Consider each of these as a chance to show your potential.

- ALWAYS have a GREAT attitude!

- Be energetic, passionate, and engaged each and every day, and help the company confirm that they made a great decision, hiring you.

- Know your company's products, business strategy, primary competitors, industry ranking, and perception in the marketplace.

- Be aware of your company's and your department's strengths and weaknesses, but be mindful of sharing your opinions on this until you have earned the right/ credibility to express your views.

- Work diligently to fit into the company culture. Do not expect them to adjust to you. Get to know your co-workers and peers . . . "Listen and learn."

- Be patient. In our current mindset quick and easy trophies, we sometimes forget that true, consistent accomplishment is the only thing that breeds career opportunities. Resist the entitlement culture. The only way to seek true accomplishments is through hard work and persistence. Instead of worrying about status, focus on what you are doing now to help your team and company to be their best.

- Do not eat lunch at your desk or by yourself. Meet your co-workers and those in other areas. Network and connect. You should eat with others as often as possible and if necessary adjust your lunch hour to allow you to connect.

- Be mindful of any commute issues or personal issues that will create time away from work. You accepted the role with the company and that means you give them your best and work around traffic delays, inconvenience, personal scheduling, and so on.

- Remember to control what you can control. Instead of getting wrapped up in what others are doing or not doing, control what you can control which is yourself. Make every effort to do your best work everyday and the rewards and career success will follow.

- Be respectful, and professional at ALL times and seek additional work during downtimes or lulls within your department.

- When asked by your boss to take on additional work, let them know you appreciate the opportunity, even if your first thought is to complain about it or say that it is unfair.

- Develop a reputation as someone who is positive, can work well with others, does not complain, and always gives their best (EVERYDAY).

- DO NOT surf the net, use your cell phone to text/call, or use the office phone to make personal e-mails during business hours.

- Most companies monitor Internet traffic and although this may sound like a "Big Brother is watching" conspiracy theory, Facebook, Internet surfing, online purchasing, or accessing inappropriate websites is regularly monitored by the company. Your boss or your boss's boss will receive notice of your online non-work activity and you will be disciplined or terminated because of it. You signed on to give your professional best for a full day's work and if you fail to do that because you are bored or for whatever non-working reason, you are in fact stealing. You are no longer giving a full day's work for a full day's pay. I know we often like gray instead of black and white, right and wrong, but if it were your company you would want everyone doing what they are getting paid to do while at work. You would not be happy if you found your newly hired or seasoned professionals participating in any non-company-related activity during company hours.

- Do NOT publicly or openly, criticize your employer, peers/ co-workers, and boss or company strategy until you fully understand all the details. You should give your best effort and trust that everyone else is doing the same. If you do not understand why someone is doing something a certain way or why they think one way is better than your way, ask them and be open-minded to evaluate their input.

- Be organized and be sure, and proof all of your work for spelling, grammar, and content multiple times before you send it to your boss or co-workers.

- Study, know, and understand emotional intelligence (EQ) and how your own EQ impacts you and the opportunities you seek in the workplace. Emotional intelligence consists of many personal attributes including your perseverance, self-control, and your ability to get along well with others. Emotional intelligence is the ability to be aware of and manage one's own emotions as well as handle the emotions of others. Your overall career success, including your day-to-day career success, will be greatly impacted by your own emotional intelligence.

- Do dress professionally at all times. Be mindful of your appearance and your BRAND. If there is an opportunity for a casual dress Friday or a more relaxed dress code do not fall to the bottom of the dress code. You can still dress on the upper end of casual. For sure, always dress appropriately. When you do not, you likely will not be taken seriously in your role.

- Be mindful of the performance aspects and results of your actions. You continue to build your resume throughout your career and by maintaining this mindset it will help you as you prepare your weekly report.

- If your company is publicly traded, actively monitor the company and industry trends and happenings via business journals, print and online media sources such as the Wall Street Journal, Bloomberg, BusinessWeek, Yahoo Finance,

Motley Fool, Google Finance, and the company website. If the company is privately held, you may have to dig a little deeper, but there are often industry associations, private company research resources such as Forbes and Fortune. You will help your personal and professional brand by being more informed. You will also be able to carry on a more intelligent business conversation with executives and others because of your research. Be informed!

- You should always stay until the job is complete and make sure it is not just "good-enough," but is in fact your BEST effort.

- Help co-workers in need. Be a great team member and team leader if the opportunity presents itself.

- Make it your personal mission to make a positive impact each and every day. Your boss, co-workers, and others will notice this and that is a legacy worth leaving.

- In your job and the workplace, be willing to push yourself and take risks. Do not be afraid to accept challenges, to face unknowns, or to deal with extensive ambiguity.

- Be willing to always go above and beyond that which is expected of you.

- Be aware of your attitude at all times. Your attitude must be "Can-Do" and positive.

- Always be professional in your communication and conduct.

- Prioritize your business e-mails and phone calls so that you respond to all relevant and business-related e-mails and phone calls within 24 hours. Work also to keep from being distracted from incoming spam, posts, or e-mails that contain jokes, political comments, and general web traffic. Not only is a 24-hour response critical for a new hire, it is also just as critical for you to meet the commitments you make via phone or e-mail. If you say you will get back to someone or have a resolution by "the end of the week" or "middle of the day tomorrow" then by all means do so, or at the very least respond to them by e-mail or phone and let them know you need to adjust your commitment and have not forgotten about them. Timely business follow-up is very important to building your brand and professional reputation.

A good book that deals with how to make a difference in your first job out of college is appropriately named: *Effective Immediately How to FIT IN, STAND OUT, and MOVE UP at Your First REAL JOB*, by Emily Bennington and Skip Lineberg. Great title, don't you think? The authors do an excellent job of profiling the critical things that you need to do in order to fit in and stand out and through these actions to "move up." The book covers 88 items that will help you make a difference and each item is brief and gives you the employer's perspective of the action.

We have had several students tell us when they started their internship or first job after graduation that the company they were employed by used the book during their incoming orientation meeting with the new employees. Even though some of the items seem like basic common sense issues, you would be surprised how many students miss out on career positioning because they did not take the advice and instruction listed in the book. The book is an easy read and you would do well to read it and add the issues and actions to what you read within this chapter. When you combine the two it will help you avoid the many unseen (and a few visible) minefields that exist as you work your way through an organization.

Final Thoughts

Your career future is in **YOUR** hands. I wish you could see how important your college experience and your first two years after graduation are to your career development. There is so much you can do in this time to realize the potential that you have. Having personal accountability for your career and addressing the issues and skill development detailed in this book will help prepare you for the competitive job market that you will face when you graduate. Pushing yourself, establishing a stronger work ethic, accepting challenges and stretch assignments, and developing your communication, leadership, and problem solving skills will give you an edge over your peers.

Most importantly, realize that YOU are the only thing that stands in the way of your success or failure. Your ATTITUDE is a critical ingredient to your career success. If you do not have an attitude already that gives you the confidence to pursue your dreams and the willingness to accept failure when you give your best, then find a way to change your heart. Enjoy each and every day and the opportunities that the day brings and know that you will be better for the challenges you face.

Never give up and never quit. You can do great things if you understand and fully buy into what it means to give your best.

Chapter 10 Review Questions

1. Preparing a brief weekly report for your boss or supervisor is a great way to insure you and your direct supervisor are in synch with your activities and priorities. It will also show you are a person who is focused on solutions and executions of the tasks, projects, and challenges you are given.

   a) True

   b) False

2. Chapter 10 spoke about some "Quick Tips" for making a GREAT impression in your new job/internship. The chapter listed over 30 tips. List the six that you think are the most important for you to use when you start your new career.

   a)

   b)

   c)

   d)

   e)

   f)

3. This chapter speaks about a critical success factor. That factor is:

   a) Your GPA.

   b) Your background.

   c) Your attitude.

   d) Understanding your needs.

   e) Work-life balance.

4. When you begin your career you should look at it as:

a) An adventure.

b) A place where what you do and how you do it speaks to your character.

c) It is not about me, it is about the positive impact I can make.

d) Five years from now will the people I work with want to recommend me to others in their career field.

e) All of the above.

CAREER RESOURCES AND LINKS

Suggested Readings

Outliers: The Story of Success, by Malcolm Gladwell
How to Interview Like a Top MBA, by Dr. Shel Leanne
The Power of Who, by Bob Beaudine
Effective Immediately: How to FIT IN, STAND OUT, and MOVE UP at Your First Real Job, by Emily Bennington and Skip Lineberg
Power Ties: The International Student's Guide to Finding a Job in the United States, by Dan Beaudry *
Extreme Ownership, by Jocko Willink and Leif Babin

Job Market Outlook

http://stats.bls.gov/ooh/

Self-Assessment Tools

www.careerleader.com
http://www.assessment.com/

Job and Internship Search Engines

> www.careershift.com
> www.indeed.com
> http://www.ajb.org/

Your college or university online recruiting portal

Case Interview Preparation

> http://www.consultingcase101.com/
> *Case in Point—Complete Case Interview Preparation* by Marc P. Cosentino
> www.casequestions.com
> *Crack the Case—How to Conquer Your Case Interviews* by David Ohrvall www.mbacase.com

Salary, Company, and Interview Research

> http://www.glassdoor.com/index.htm
> www.salary.com
> www.payscale.com

Cost of Living Comparison

> http://www.bestplaces.net/cost-of-living/

Company Research

> http://fortune.com/fortune500/

General Career Tools

> http://www.careerinfonet.org/crl/library.aspx

Resume and Applicant Tracking System Support

http://www.hireright.com/blog/2013/11/meet-the-robots-reading-your-resume-infographic-ats-recruiting/